The Book of
Bideford

The Development of a Devonian Market Town

PETER CHRISTIE & ALISON GRANT

First published in Great Britain in 2005

British Library Cataloguing-in-Publication Data.
A CIP record for this title is available from the British Library.

ISBN 1 84114 405 3

HALSGROVE

Halsgrove House
Lower Moor Way
Tiverton, Devon EX16 6SS
Tel: 01884 243242
Fax: 01884 243325
email: sales@halsgrove.com
website: www.halsgrove.com

Title page photograph: *This print by H. Besley, from c.1860, shows a ship on the stocks near the bridge. The now-demolished Silver Street chapel looms above St Mary's Church.* (PC)

Printed and bound in Great Britain by CPI Bath.

Little White Town

*A*ll who have travelled through the delicious scenery of North Devon must needs know the little white town of Bideford, which slopes upwards from its broad tide-river paved with yellow sand and many-arched old bridge where salmon wait for Autumn floods, toward the pleasant upland on the west. Above the town the hills close in, cushioned with deep oak woods, through which juts here and there a crag of fern-fringed slate; below they lower, and open more and more in softly rounded knolls, and fertile squares of red and green, till they sink into the wide expanse of hazy flats, rich salt marshes, and rolling sand hills where Torridge joins her sister Taw, and both together flow quietly toward the broad surges of the bar and the everlasting thunder of the long Atlantic swell. Pleasantly the old town stands there, beneath its soft Italian sky, fanned day and night by the fresh ocean breeze, which forbids alike the keen winter frosts, and the fierce thunder heats of the midlands; and pleasantly it has stood there for now, perhaps eight hundred years...

Charles Kingsley – *Westward Ho!* (1855)

Acknowledgements

Putting the materials together for this book has been a real pleasure in that everyone we have approached has been so helpful and encouraging. We would like to thank all of them, especially the staff of the North Devon Athenaeum, the North Devon Record Office, the Bideford Library and Bob and Ann Brock. We are also grateful to those who have loaned photographs or ephemera, especially Mary Cleaver whose late husband Dick was so far-sighted in saving what others have thrown away. Owners of photographs are as follows:

JB	John Baker
CB	Cyril Barfoot
AB	Arthur Blamey
BB	Barbara Bowring
GB	Graham Braddick
RC	Roger Cann
PC	Peter Christie
HC	Dick Cleaver
JC	Jean Couch
RD	R. Davies
PF	Peter Ferguson
DF	Douglas French
CH	Christian Havemeyer
VH	Vanessa Heard
JJ	J. Jenn
RLK	R.L. Knight
LM	Louise Martin
MM	Mark Myers
SO	S. Oke
WP	William Passmore
MP	Morgan Photographic
BP	Basil Pidgeon
AP	Alice Prust
MS	Michael Schiller
PS	Pat Slade
DT	Des Taylor
PU	Pam Underhill
AV	Andrew Vanstone
AW	Audrey Woodyatt
BARC	Bideford Amateur Rowing Club
BBT	Bideford Bridge Trust
BL	Bideford Library
BTC	Bideford Town Council
NDA	North Devon Athenaeum
NDMT	North Devon Museum Trust
NDRO	North Devon Record Office
NDDCRAU	North Devon District Council Rescue Archaeology Unit
NDJ	North Devon Journal
PRO	Public Record Office
RAMM	Royal Albert Memorial Museum.

Contents

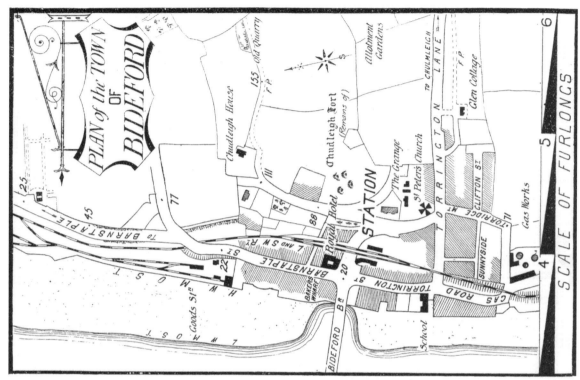

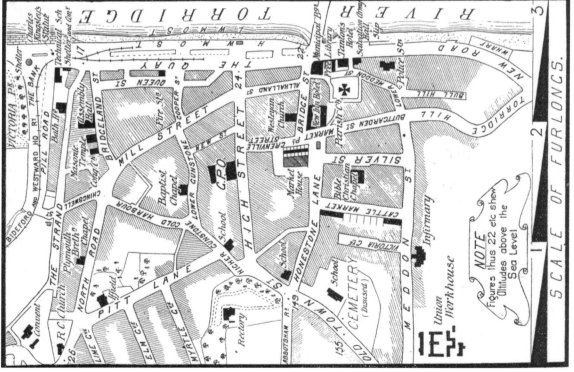

Maps of Bideford from a 1920s guidebook showing many of the sites mentioned in this book. (PC)

Chapter 1

Foundations

Bideford's physical development and history have been determined by its dry, well-drained site at the lowest practical crossing place of a navigable river. Hills to the west shelter it from the fury of Atlantic gales, and the soil is easily worked. 'The town lyeth on the side of a Hill' wrote a seventeenth-century visitor; the highest point seen by people entering Bideford from the east, across the old bridge, is called Mount Pleasant – a name which could also be applied to the site of the town.

The main part of Bideford is situated on a small knoll on the west side of the River Torridge, where it begins to narrow. Meddon and Grenville Streets, Lime Grove, North Road, Mill and Allhalland Streets almost encircle this knoll, while High and Bridge Streets, Pitt Lane, Coldharbour and Honestone rise precipitately from them, converging at Old Town. Geologically, alluvial deposits define the extent of the pills (creeks) marking the northern boundary of the town on both sides of the river. These formed 'with the addition of the tide a very broad sheet of water' before reclamation and road schemes in the nineteenth and twentieth centuries. Occasionally the water has returned to claim its old areas, channels leading to floods in low-lying areas.

When the central pier of the Bideford bypass bridge was sunk into the bed of the Torridge, bone, horn, twigs and hazelnuts were recovered from the lowest levels, indicating that 10,000 or more years ago the area was covered by forest. This was later submerged, as at nearby Westward Ho!, where similar remains are exposed at low tides. Considerable numbers of flint flakes and scrapers from the Middle Stone Age (8000–4000BC) have been found further up the river valley, suggesting that early man used it as a route and hunted in the area. Flint artefacts were also brought up from below the riverbed, together with a fine polished stone axe, from the New Stone Age (4000–2500BC). In the town itself, any prehistoric remains are likely to have been destroyed or overlaid by subsequent development, but there is always the exciting possibility that archaeological excavation will reveal more evidence of Bideford's remote past.

By the time of the Roman conquest, Devon had been occupied by Celtic tribes, builders of 'iron age' hill-forts. In the neighbouring parish of Alverdiscott, a Roman temporary 'marching camp' of the first century AD has been identified alongside one of these earthworks, but it is not known if there was fighting in the neighbourhood, or just that Roman troops advanced westwards to ford the Torridge. Roman coins have occasionally been found in the town and parish, so it is possible that the river crossing brought trade to the site in Roman times. Most of the Celtic population probably made a living by farming, or fishing the often-turbulent river, whose name, Torridge, comes from their word meaning violent or rough.

The Saxons began their conquest of Devon in the late-seventh century, enslaving the Celts or driving them westwards, and giving their own names to the land they occupied. Thus an obscure Saxon, Byda, achieved a kind of immortality when he gave his name to the ford near which he settled. Many other Saxon names are found in Bideford parish. Adjavin, for instance, was once 'Ecga fen', 'the fen belonging

A view down High Street from about 1870, showing the wide variation in building styles that developed over the centuries. (PC)

Occasionally the River Torridge reasserts its old course and here, in a photograph from November 1939, we see the Kenwith Valley under water – thus re-establishing the waterway possibly used by the Vikings to attack Kenwith Castle. (PC)

Alexandra Terrace in the Kenwith Valley under water in the 1950s. (PC)

We have no illustrations of Bideford before the eighteenth century but in 1925 the Bideford Bridge Trust widened the bridge and to celebrate a Historical Pageant was held when several hundred townspeople dressed up as historical characters in the town's history. This photograph shows the coronation of William the Conqueror. William was played by Arthur Chope with Miss Lord playing Queen Matilda, the first Norman owner of Bideford. (RLK)

to Edgar'. Old Town from 'ton', meaning enclosure or farm, indicates an early settlement; Moreton means 'the farm on the moor', and Gammaton could derive from 'gafol manna ton', meaning 'a farm inhabited by men who paid gavel or rent to an overlord'. These and other farms were worked by Saxons; some of them may be on earlier Celtic sites. Other Saxons would have farmed strips scattered over large open fields adjoining a central settlement, a method of cultivation now known to have been more extensive in Devon than was once thought. Maps made as late as the nineteenth century show, to the west and north of the town, the remains of an extensive strip system, cultivated by generations of Bideford smallholders for over 1,000 years.

Left: *A fine 'greenstone' axe from the bed of the River Torridge, found when the new Torridge bridge was being built. Similar axes have been found on New Stone Age sites in Cornwall, Brittany and many other places.* (PC)

Below: *A report from the* North Devon Journal *of May 1830 relating to a rare example of a Roman presence in North Devon. Mr Tyeth's estate was at East-the-Water around Pillmouth.*

BIDEFORD.—On Monday, the Magistrates fined several shopkeepers for having weights short of the standard, of whom one was fined ten and another fifteen shillings.

On Thursday last, a Roman Coin was found on the estate of W. S. Tyeth, Esq. of the reign of the Emperor A. Vitellius Germanicus, in a very fine state of preservation, being now 1751 years old.

APPLEDORE. — On Saturday the 24th ultimo, was launched from the shipbuilding yard of Mr. Clibbett, sen. a fine Smack, about 46 tons register, and will burthen

The Saxon invaders became peaceful farmers, only to be threatened in their turn by the Vikings, sailing up rivers and creeks in their longships, in search of plunder. In 878, in Alfred the Great's time, a fleet of 23 ships under Hubba the Dane entered the Bristol Channel and, as a chronicler wrote, 'many of the king's servants or officers retired with their followers and shut themselves up for safety in the castle of Cynuit.' It has been suggested that this was at Countisbury, but there is also a strong tradition that it was at Kenwith, just over the boundary into Northam, and only a mile from the centre of Bideford. The Vikings are generally believed to have left their ships on the banks of the Torridge, two or three miles below Bideford, but they could have brought some at least as far as the settlement, to sail up the long tidal pill. This would explain why the Saxons either made use of a fort already on the site, or themselves constructed the mound and other earthworks known as Kenwith Castle, to guard the route inland from the head of the pill. Under Odun, Earl of Devon, they drove the Vikings from the high ground back to their ships; 1,200 of the enemy were killed, including the leader. Beside the Torridge, above Appledore, a large slab known as the Hubbastone (now lost, due to nineteenth-century development) was believed to mark his last resting place. If Kenwith was indeed Cynuit, there could be some truth in this tradition and men from Bideford, having successfully defended their homes, would have witnessed the funeral rites beside the river.

On the successful Norman invasion of 1066, Brictric, the Saxon lord of Bideford, lost it to William I's queen, Matilda. The manor, or estate, passed to the king after her death in 1083, three years before the Domesday survey. In eleventh-century Bideford the king, as lord of the manor, had a tenant to work the demesne or home farm. This was at Ford, one of the earliest and most important sites, with lands

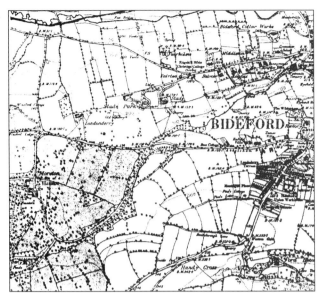

The remains of strip cultivation can still be discerned to the west of the town on this map of 1886. Many of the old field names are commemorated in the road names on the Londonderry housing estate which covers this area at the time of writing. (PC)

which until quite recently extended northwards as far as Meddon Street, the boundary line between the demesne and the riverside settlement. The fine old house at Ford, the most ancient local farmstead, would have been built on the site of an even earlier one. The Domesday survey recorded 14 slaves on the demesne land, using four ploughs, and tending 18 cattle and 300 sheep.

The Domesday Book also recorded 20 more ploughs used by the rest of the farmers. There were 30 villeins or tenant farmers, and eight cottagers, too many for each man to have his own plough and individual farm. Those with outlying farms almost certainly had their own ploughs, while the rest shared the remaining ploughs on their strips of land behind the settlement on the west bank of the Torridge. Ten acres of meadow, 20 of pasture and 150 acres of woodland were recorded at Bideford, and a fishery worth 25 shillings a year in 1066. Some men were fishermen, and others craftsmen or traders.

Ford House, one of the oldest buildings in Bideford, was probably the demesne house (home farm) of the lords of the manor. (PC)

The Domesday Book entry for 'Bedeford' from 1086. The fourth line shows that the manor was valued at £16 a year, with a piscaria (fishery) worth 25s. (£1.25). (NDA)

Bideford was not among the richest and most populous Devon manors but, with 52 men and their families, and a value of £16 a year, it was well above the average, and could, as it was then recorded, have supported two more ploughs.

Domesday surveyors, ordered to assess land values for taxation purposes, asked set questions and recorded the answers of Saxon elders. There is no indication that anyone in 1086 saw the manor of 'Bedeford' as a potential thriving town and port.

Above: *Londonderry estate in its very earliest form, showing the long, narrow fields and ancient field hedges. The Slade area is in the centre of the photograph.* (PC)

Below: *The fishery lasted until well into the late-twentieth century as this photograph, which dates from the 1970s, shows.* (HC)

9

This aerial photograph from around 1927 gives a good impression of what the early town must have looked like. Kingsley Road has just been built. (AP)

Right: *A steelpoint print of the bridge published in 1830 is still recognisable in the early-twenty-first century. Note that both sides of the river were being used for berthing vessels.* (PC)

Left: *The Kingsley Hotel to the left of this picture stood on the site owned by the merchant John Hooper in the fifteenth century. The pillory stood opposite.* (PS)

Chapter 2

Borough and Bridge

Soon after the Domesday survey, the manor of Bideford passed to Richard de Granville (or Grenville) whose descendants held it until the eighteenth century. The early Grenvilles, following the example of many twelfth-century lords of Devon manors, created a borough on their land, in the hope of increasing their income by promoting trade. In the borough of Bideford, men who could pay the lord twelve pence a year for a burgage plot of six acres, or sixpence for a house and orchard, became burgesses, free from many of the old dues and services. Richard Grenville, a thirteenth-century lord of the manor, promised Bideford much the same liberties as Bristol, in a charter confirming a grant made by his grandfather. Through this earlier grant Bideford had achieved borough status perhaps before 1200, and certainly by 1238, when it was among 18 boroughs that sent burgesses to meet the justices of assize, or travelling judges, when they came to Devon.

The burgesses paid Richard Grenville four marks of silver (£2.66) for his charter, which increased their freedom and prosperity. Common pasture for their beasts was one of the rights confirmed, showing that the rural way of life remained important. It is clear that Bideford was also a place of considerable trade, with a weekly market. Described by Richard Grenville as 'my Monday market', this had probably been founded by an earlier lord, as the first step towards the creation of the borough; Grenville retained the profits, although he freed the burgesses from tolls at other markets and fairs on his lands. The lord also retained 'suit of court', whereby all

Bideford's Manor Court, dating from medieval times, is held with due ceremony once a year. Here, in 1987, the Mayor Pam Paddon supervises with the late Ian Hay, the then town clerk, sitting below her. (MP)

burgesses had to attend his monthly court, or pay a fine. The Tuesday after Michaelmas was a special 'lawday', when the burgesses elected one of their number to serve as head officer or reeve. His main duty was to collect all taxes and tolls, which the town was now allowed to keep in return for an annual payment of 10s. Bideford Manor Court survived long after the medieval period, and at the time of writing still meets once a year, enabling ratepayers to air grievances or make suggestions to the Town Council, which bought out the last lord of the manor in 1882.

A tax assessment of 1332 shows that there were then 30 burgesses in Bideford, paying sums ranging from 8d. to 10s. One of them was John le Hopere (or Hooper), who paid 3s. – about the average. The chance survival of a bundle of old deeds makes it possible to follow the fortunes of his family in the fourteenth and fifteenth centuries. The first document, dated 1342, mentions 'the street called Mill Street'. A town mill would have been a priority, once the people were free from the obligation to use the lord's. Unfortunately there are no maps of medieval Bideford to show its whereabouts. There were many later mills along the Pill, and in the late-eighteenth century there was still a tidemill near its confluence with the Torridge. In medieval times there could have been a tidemill at the bottom of Mill Street, which was just beyond the end of the Quay in those days.

The Hooper family's holdings increased until, in 1420, another John Hooper inherited many 'burgages, lands and tenements' in Bideford, 'with houses, closes and appurtenances of all kinds thereto belonging.' If he left no children, these properties were to go to his sister, which is probably what happened. When he died that same year, he left 20 dozen lengths of woollen cloth for distribution to the poor. This strongly suggests that he, and probably his predecessors, were in the cloth trade, on which the fortunes of many Devon merchants and towns in the Middle Ages were founded. For the export of Bideford cloth and the import of return cargoes such as French wine, John Hooper would have used the *Grace de Dieu*, a ship of which he was part-owner. He bequeathed his share in the vessel to a relative, Walter Hooper, who also received John's best cloak, a blue gown lined with green cloth, one doublet, one hauberk or coat of mail, and a bassinet or helmet 'with rerebrace and vambrace'. Other bequests included two striped gowns, a lined blue gown, a cloth robe, a gown lined with deerskin, and a dagger.

A photograph of the interior of the old bonded warehouse owned by Wickham's in Lower Gunstone taken in 1959. The barrels containing wines and spirits would have been a common sight in early Bideford. The building, which was built in 1837, has since been converted into flats. (BP)

Where in Bideford did John Hooper live? In 1399–1400 his father, William, had acquired two adjacent properties in the High Street. The scribe, using Latin, the language of legal documents, wrote that one was 'on the north part of the High Street' then added the two English words 'atte corner' before continuing in Latin, 'with the street called Mylstret on the east part.' This description makes it possible to identify both properties, so John Hooper owned the sites occupied in 2004 by New Look and the adjoining travel agent. The deeds of the second property show that it was opposite the pillory, a feature which often occupied a central place in medieval towns. There must therefore have been a public open space, perhaps a market-place, somewhere near the junction of High Street with Allhalland Street, 'the street of all saints'. This was then the only way to and from the end of the bridge, where there was a chapel of the same name. John Hooper therefore lived at the hub of the town. At the bottom of High Street was the Quay, with its 'tome stone', on which payments and binding agreements were made without recourse to pen and paper.

The medieval Quay stood farther back than it does in the twenty-first century, so that the carved stone, built into the corner of the shop at the bottom of High Street, may once have been the column of 'the Broade Stone standing upon the Kaye of Bydeforde,' as a document from 1587 describes it.

In spite of his wealth, John Hooper's life was probably unhappy, and his wife's even more so, as an entry in the Bishop of Exeter's register of 1421 shows. John Walhoppe, the new rector of Bideford, refused to bury anyone in his churchyard, which he considered had been defiled because Matilda, John Hooper's widow, who 'had been guilty of suicide by hanging herself', had been buried there. An enquiry showed that Matilda had for some time been 'notoriously insane', so could not be held responsible. The rector must have known of Matilda's condition, for her husband's will left her the household goods on condition that she was 'in quiet and peace' with his executors, one of whom

was John Walhoppe himself. He was ordered to resume burials. John Hooper, who had left him 20s., was a great benefactor of Bideford Church. He bequeathed money for masses and lights for the altar, arranged for goods to be sold to pay the salary of a priest for four years or more, and left £10 for the restoration of the church tower.

The tower is almost all that survives of Bideford's medieval church. When the rest was pulled down in 1862, remains of an earlier building were reported, and a Saxon foundation has been claimed. This, although possible, has not been proved, and the only survival from an earlier church is the Norman font. The next church was dedicated to St Mary, by Bishop Bronescombe of Exeter in 1259. Pious and prosperous townsmen left money for additions, repairs, masses, and memorials. Sir Thomas Grenville, who died in 1513, left money to endow a chantry, and a priest 'to sing there and pray for me and myn auncestors and heires for ever.' His splendid monument, with an effigy in full armour, is one of the few to survive the nineteenth-century rebuilding. Bideford Church, built and rebuilt in periods of prosperity, is

Allhalland Street in the 1920s. This street, mentioned in fourteenth-century deeds, was the main entrance to the town before the Quay was extended to the bridge.

The High Street is unusually wide between the site of John Hooper's house and the Quay, and was probably the town's market-place in medieval times.

A photograph of four 'Crusaders' from the 1925 Historical Pageant. The two on the right have been identified as Jack Meredith and R. Braund. (RLK)

probably on land given by one of his predecessors, for it was founded where the borough adjoined the demesne and, like the bridge nearby, was in a good position to serve both.

'Everyone who knows Bideford, cannot but know Bideford Bridge' wrote Charles Kingsley, who continued, tongue-in-cheek:

> *... for it is the very... soul around which the town, as a body, has organised itself... being first an inspired bridge; a soul-saving bridge; an alms-giving bridge; an educational bridge; a sentient bridge; and last but not least, a dinner-giving bridge.*

According to the account of John Leland the antiquary, written between 1534 and 1543, the work was 'inspired' when:

> *... a poor Preste began thys Bridge: and as it is said, he was animatid so to do by a vision. Then al the Cuntrey about sette their Handes onto the performing of it...*

The vision perhaps provided a powerful argument for a site conveniently near the church! Another account

names the priest as Richard Gurnard, which adds substance to the legend, only if it is supposed that the bridge was founded before 1257, for he is not mentioned in the Bishops' registers which survive from that time onwards. An early date for the first bridge is possible, for neither market nor borough could have flourished for long without it. A later foundation is suggested, however, by a somewhat tenuous tradition that Peter Quivil, Bishop of Exeter from 1280 to 1291, was the first to grant 'soul-saving' indulgences to those who contributed towards the 'forwarding' of the bridge. It certainly existed by 1327, when Bishop Stapleton left 40s. to 'the bridge of Bydeforde'.

Bideford bridge is noted for its 24 arches of different widths, once thought to have been due to varying sums given by rich merchants or surrounding parishes for its foundation, but now known to correspond to the size of the timbers of the original. The uprights of each wooden arch were linked by slanting supports to the lintel, enabling widths of 12 to 25 feet to be achieved. Indulgences of 1396 and later, mentioning both construction and repair, probably refer to the stone bridge built to encase the wooden one, although it is not known when this work was

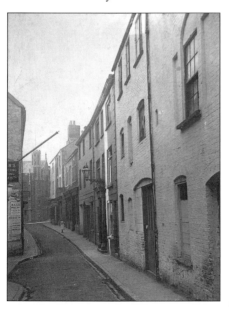

Left: Allhalland Street, the main entrance into Bideford for many centuries, photographed c.1890. Note the short section of widened road – an initiative by the Town Council to make the road easier to traverse – which came to nothing in the end. (BL)

Right: This stone, now built into the corner of a shop at the junction of High Street and the Quay, may have been the column of the 'tome stone' which was used for the transaction of business. (PC)

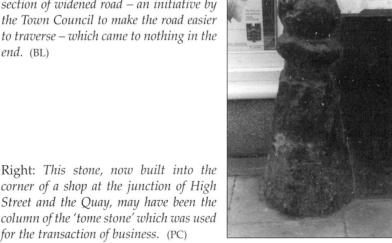

This aerial view dates from the 1930s and clearly shows how the western part of the town has grown up and away from the Quay and bridge. (HC)

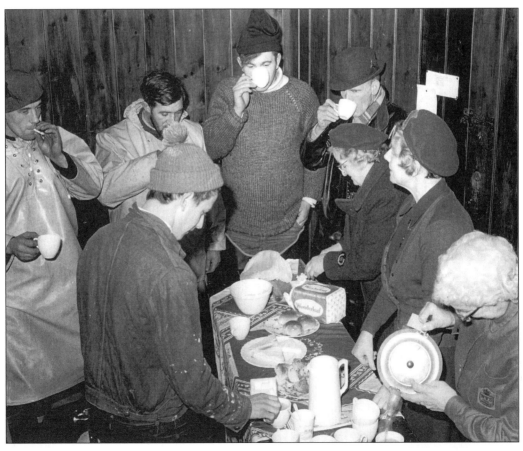

In January 1968 the two western-most arches of Bideford bridge collapsed and the town was thrown into chaos. A pedestrian ferry was quickly laid on and here we see members of the WRVS serving tea to the ferrymen. The ladies are, left to right: *Ada Lee, Eileen Turner and Mrs Gilson.* (HC)

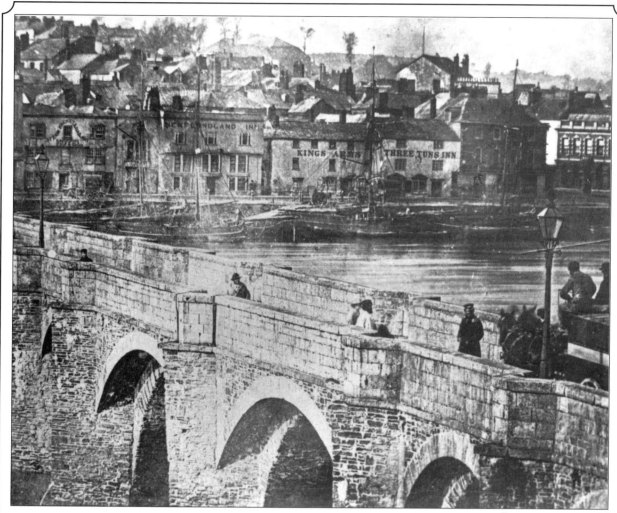

Above: *A classic view of Bideford's famous old bridge. This rather poor photograph is one of the earliest views of the town and was taken c.1863. The indented stone parapet has long gone but the arches still remain. The four public houses on the Quay are now reduced to just one.* (PC)

Above left and right: *Access to the town was hampered by the narrow roads approaching both ends of the bridge. In one photograph from c.1920 we see Barnstaple Street, East-the-Water, just before it reached the bridge end.* (JB) *The other, looking down the same street in the opposite direction, shows a building front being taken down to widen the road around the turn of the nineteenth century.* (PC)

A later aerial view from the 1960s shows a much-developed town, but the dominant position of the bridge is still very apparent. (HC)

carried out. Theobald Grenville is sometimes credited with finishing the bridge in the mid-fourteenth century, but the work could have begun earlier. The 'custodians of the goods of the bridge of Bideford', later known as the Bridge Trust, were soon receiving rents – for instance 2s. a year from John Hooper who, like many other burgesses, also left a bequest to the bridge when he died. The Bridge Trust, over the centuries, used its considerable resources not only for the purposes noted by Kingsley, but to develop the town itself. Its first care, however, had always to be the 677-feet-long bridge, which, although not literally founded on bags of wool as sometimes claimed, was as remarkable an achievement in its day as the new Torridge bridge in ours. For 700 years or more it withstood tide and tempest before, mainly due to a weight of traffic its builders could not have foreseen, part of it collapsed in 1968. Then, cut off, people realised the importance of the bridge in transporting goods, as a link between the two halves of the town, and why their forefathers built it, to ensure the growth and prosperity of the town.

Between 1150 and 1350 the population of Devon increased, and great economic development took place. More land was brought into cultivation, and boroughs – the new towns of the period – were deliberately created, leading to increased food production, the expansion of sheep rearing and the cloth trade, and much building. This was the background against which Bideford developed. First came the lord's grants of market and borough, then probably a town

mill and, unless it already existed, an early church, all achieved by or soon after 1200, by which time the first wooden bridge possibly spanned the Torridge.

Another period of urban expansion in the later-thirteenth century was marked, first by a bigger church, then a new borough charter, and then or later by the cladding of the bridge in stone, with a chapel at each end. The Black Death of 1348 was a setback, but John Hooper's prosperity is an indication that, in Bideford as in Devon generally, the cloth trade and shipbuilding had recovered by the early-fifteenth century. Bideford's later economic progress rested on the solid foundations laid in the medieval period.

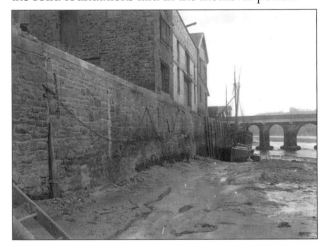

The wharves at East-the-Water just after the 1925 bridge widening, showing the ever-present mudbanks and the differing widths of the arches. (BL)

16

Chapter 3

New Worlds for Old

Charles Kingsley's 'most ruthless, bloodthirsty book', *Westward Ho!*, begins in 1575, with the hero, Amyas Leigh, a schoolboy on Bideford Quay, listening avidly to men 'who had picked the lock of the New World.' Kingsley, who completed his famous book in the six months he spent in the town in 1854, fired the imagination of thousands with his vision of Bideford's stirring past. His statue at the end of the Quay is a well-known landmark, but how many visitors, or even townspeople, see the small brass tablet in the church in memory of Sir Richard Grenville, the real hero of Elizabethan Bideford?

Richard Grenville was only three years old when his father, the captain of the *Mary Rose*, went down with his ship in Portsmouth Harbour in 1545. When his grandfather died five years later, the young Richard became lord of the manor of Bideford. He married Mary, the daughter of Sir John St Leger of Annery, a near neighbour, whose family held land and high position in Ireland. Grenville became interested in establishing an English settlement there, and was appointed Sheriff of Cork. In 1569 an Irish rebellion ended his plans, and he was among those who savagely put it down and laid waste the land. This venture had important consequences for Bideford; townsmen who had followed Grenville as soldiers or would-be settlers, and sailors who had manned his ships, had begun to forge links with southern Ireland, which were to play an important part in the expansion of trade.

John Leland had reported earlier in the century that there was no longer a set market-day at Bideford and, soon after Grenville's return from Ireland, there were complaints about the expense of maintaining the bridge. It was also said that:

> *... by the number of near neighbours and multitudes coming thither from all parts, it is greatly impoverished and standeth full of people... and for want of such liberties and privileges which other antient boroughs have... the said village of Bedyford is made to decline into poverty.*

Like other towns at the time, Bideford sought to shake off feudal restrictions and run its own affairs, and Grenville, who found Bideford an ideal base for his expeditions, wisely decided to join the merchants, rather than fight them. The alliance thus created served Bideford well. The townsmen agreed to confirm a number of Grenville's rights, and in return he secured a charter from Elizabeth I in 1574. This

Charles Kingsley's statue at the end of the Quay. His book Westward Ho! *uses Elizabethan Bideford as its setting – and later gave its name to a nearby tourist resort. The statue was paid for by public subscription and erected in 1906.* (PC)

raised Bideford to the status of a corporation with a mayor, five aldermen, seven 'capital' burgesses, and its own Justice of the Peace, chosen annually from the aldermen. John Salterne, a merchant, was chosen as the first mayor, and Grenville served as an alderman. A court of record was set up, with a recorder, town clerk and two sergeants-at-mace. The charter also provided a Tuesday market, three annual fairs, and a sound basis for Bideford's economic progress during the next century.

The idea of 'planting' settlers remained in Grenville's mind, and in 1574 he proposed to 'found a settlement on the River Plate, and then pass the Strait [of Magellan] and establish settlements...' The Queen agreed, then fearing trouble with Spain, changed her mind, so the expedition never set out. In 1585, however, Sir Walter Raleigh involved Grenville, a

Left: *An old engraving of Sir Richard Grenville.* (PC)

The emblems of the town – its silver maces. The smaller probably dates from 1573 and the larger from the Charles I period (1625–49). They are still ceremoniously carried by the beadles at civic events. (PC)

The borough beadles holding the maces in 1985. Borough status was confirmed and a court of record granted by a charter of Elizabeth I in 1574. (MP)

A photograph of Silver Street looking towards the post-1884 market, showing just how narrow the early streets could be. (BL)

'Raleigh' could have resembled the Indian shown here and have lived in this kind of village. The artist, John White, who had been to Roanoke with Grenville in 1585, was in Bideford in 1588, expecting to join another expedition to Virginia. (BL)

distant relative, in his schemes to plant a colony in Virginia. Grenville commanded the expedition which took the first colonists to Roanoke Island in what is now North Carolina, and led a party which explored the surrounding area. On his return he ensured a profit on the voyage when he took a valuable Spanish prize, leading the boarding party 'with a boate made with boards of chests, which fell asunder, and sunke at the ship's side, as soone as ever he and his men were out of it.' This ship, the *Santa Maria de San Vicente*, may have been the large vessel which could not negotiate Bideford bar on a neap tide, when the next expedition set out for Roanoke. Adam Wyatt, town clerk of Barnstaple, wrote in his diary in 1586:

16th April... Sir Richard Greynvylle sailed over the barr with his flee boat [fly boat] *and friget, but for want of sufficient water on the barr being neare upon neape, he left his ship. This Sir Richard Greynvylle pretended* [intended] *his going to Wyngandecora, where he was last year.*

This delay proved unfortunate, but Grenville also took his time on the way, capturing or plundering a number of vessels by virtue of official letters of reprisal which licensed privately-owned ships as 'privateers'. One of his prizes was a French vessel carrying Spanish wine and oil, which he sent back to Bideford. The expedition at last arrived at Roanoke with reinforcements and stores, only to find the colony abandoned, the hard-pressed settlers having returned home with Sir Francis Drake, who had passed that way a few weeks earlier. Grenville left 15 men to hold the island and went off in search of

further prizes. His return to Bideford was noted by Adam Wyatt; 'In December this year (1586) Sir Richard Greynfild came home bringing a prise with him, laden with sugar, ginger and hyds [hides].' A successful voyage? The men left at Roanoke were later attacked by Indians, driven off the island, and never heard of again.

Some of the early colonists may well have been from Bideford, like many of Grenville's seamen. He had brought back a native, a 'Wynganditoian', who was christened 'Raleigh' at St Mary's on 27 March 1588, possibly in the presence of his namesake. John White, noted for his drawings of the people, plants and animals of Virginia, was also in Bideford that spring, arranging supplies and more settlers for the 'City of Ralegh', which he had set up the previous year. Grenville had an expedition ready to sail, but was ordered to take his ships to Plymouth, to strengthen the fleet against the expected Spanish Armada. A dozen or so settlers, including White, set out from Bideford aboard the *Brave* and the *Roe*, ships too small for the fleet. Interested mainly in profit, the crews plundered first a Scottish then a Breton ship. The *Brave* was then attacked by a large French vessel from La Rochelle, 'God justly punishing us for our former thievery,' as White wrote. After a grim struggle, with some loss of life, the *Brave* just managed to limp back to Bideford, and the *Roe*, which had gone off in pursuit of another prize, also abandoned the voyage, so no settlers or supplies reached Virginia that year.

Although Bideford, like other West Country seaports, was profiting by barely-legalised piracy, colonising voyages were expected at least to pay for themselves. Raleigh hoped his settlement would provide a base for privateering, and the Queen

Above: *Sir Francis Drake (F. Bishop) walks beside Queen Elizabeth (Miss Boyd) across the newly-widened bridge in 1925 as part of the associated celebrations.* (RLK)

Below: *Bideford parish registers show the baptism in 1588 and the burial the following year of 'Raleigh', an American Indian brought to England by Sir Richard Grenville.* (NDRO)

Originally entitled *'Sir Francis Drake plays bowls on Plymouth Hoe,'* this photograph taken on the Sports Ground features F. Bishop (far left) as Drake with H. Meredith (far right) as Sir Richard Grenville. Also present are R. Dymond, G. Turner, F. Upton, W. Jordan and D. Leonard. (RLK)

Few would recognise this scene today. It is the corner of Silver and Meddon Street. F.C. Squire advertises as a 'Practical Bootmaker' whose work is 'Neatly executed', whilst his window carries posters for entertainments, including the melodrama Maria Martin, *in the Bideford Public Rooms.* (BL)

Silver Street looking towards Meddon Street. The steps have long disappeared and the frontages of the houses have been greatly changed since this photograph was taken c.1900. Try to spot the man up a ladder, probably checking the burners in the gas lamp. (BL)

contributed if there was a chance of profit. Grenville and the Bideford men who followed him were not alone in seeking a return for risking ships and lives, and thus allowing the pursuit of prizes to take precedence over colonisation. The consequences, however, were tragic for, when White returned to Virginia in 1590, he found no trace of the settlers he had left, who included his daughter, her husband, and their baby daughter, Virginia Dare, the first English child to be born there. Sir Richard Grenville, in spite of his intentions, did not return to the settlement after 1586, and Bideford played no further part in these colonising ventures. The Indian, Raleigh, the 'free forest wanderer', died and was buried in Bideford in 1589, 'a sort of emblem,' wrote Kingsley, 'of the sad fate of that worn out Red race to whom civilization came too late to save.'

Bideford's prosperity was not based solely on privateering. Port records of the later-sixteenth century show a growing export of woollen cloth. Some merchants traded with La Rochelle in France, but the richest, William Andrew, mainly traded with Spain, shipping cloth out and bringing back valuable cargoes of Spanish iron. The Andrew family was an interesting one in several ways, for not only did they engage in all the main trades of Bideford, as will be seen, but after William's death in 1575 his widow, Sybil, traded in her own name, until she too died in 1590. By this time her son, John, later a benefactor to the poor of Bideford, was old enough to carry on the family's trades. On the very day of her death she made her will, from which we can learn much about life in sixteenth-century Bideford. Unlike the wills of many Bidefordians, who were more interested in bequeathing money or the leases of their land (which

Jubilee Square, c.1900, with what looks like a very early petrol pump in front of the fenced in bushes. The 'Local Board' refers to Bideford Town Council. This open space on the Quay would have been used for the temporary storage of shipping goods prior to their loading or movement to the many warehouses surrounding this area. (BL)

of course brought in money), she more or less was giving mementoes to those dear to her. Like Shakespeare she knew the value of beds, but unlike him it was her best feather bed which she named in her bequest to a daughter, another Sybil. She also left beds to her son, George, and to her daughter, Edie Ching. Chests, especially of cypress, were also valuable enough to be distinguished in Sybil's will, for perhaps they had the right sort of smell for keeping clothes or linen. She left one to her son, John, with instructions it was to be passed on to a grandson, William, the son of William, her dead son, and two to other grandsons, John and Andrewe. Barnard Shurt, probably the youngest grandson, had to make do with an 'oaken' chest, but it was the best one!

People in Elizabethan times reckoned they were well off if they had numerous pans of brass or other metal, and Sybil Andrew was no exception. She left her best pan to a son-in-law, a red brass pan to a grandson, a white brass pan to a granddaughter, and her best kettle to her daughter, Edie. For the rest, a gold ring, 'gobletts', a gilt tankard, silver salts (cellars) and spoons were mentioned, and even a best coverlet. She also left about £60 in money, a considerable amount in those days, and a house at East-the-Water. This will tells us what was important to a rich woman of those days. Sybil had no real need to provide for her children, for they were all married and doing well or reasonably so, but she must have wanted to leave them something. Her son, William Andrew, had been one of several North Devon men who worked (and died) in Cadiz before the war with Spain. His job was to sell cloth and ship return cargoes – Seville oil and white salt, for example. He also marketed fish brought by Bideford ships from Newfoundland.

Established in the sixteenth century, Bideford's Newfoundland trade increased in the seventeenth

In 1956 the North Devon Journal-Herald *featured this photograph of a so-called 'Elizabethan anchor' in Bideford. In fact, it dates from the early-nineteenth century.* (NDJ)

The Quay widening in 1889–90 led to the removal of some old cannon which had been used as mooring posts. Said to have been found on the local sandbank, Graysands, at the time of writing they are in Victoria Park. The Octagon bandstand can clearly be seen in the background. (BL)

This photograph dates from January 1956 and shows the Andrew Dole Charity being handed out in the Mayor's Parlour in the Town Hall. This was set up under the will of John Andrew in 1605. In the photograph Deputy Mayor C. Cann, assisted by the Mayor's Secretary Miss J. Bedingfield, hands out loaves of bread. Andrew's largesse continues today with cash payments having replaced the bread 'dole'. (NDJ)

Bideford's so-called 'Armada Chest'. These chests were usually made in Nuremburg in the seventeenth century and had nothing to do with the Spanish Armada. Bideford's chest was kept in the Customs House to hold revenue and was screwed to the floor. At the time of writing it is in the North Devon Maritime Museum at Appledore. (PC)

Above: Various 'Tudor' and 'Elizabethan' women outside a building in Torrington Street, East-the-Water. Included in the group are: J. Short, J. Ash, G. Turner, R. Boyle, O. Davey, B. Perkins, M. Jewell, G. Shepherd, M. Andrew and E. Meredith. On the far right is Mrs E. Leonard, one of the two wardrobe mistresses for the whole bridge widening pageant in 1925. (RLK)

Right: Queen Street looking towards the 2004 site of HSBC bank in 1897. The cobbles have long gone – or probably been tarmaced over, whilst the splendid gas lamp has also disappeared. At one time these buildings would have faced the Quay – indeed the old Quay wall lies under the back wall of the HSBC bank. (RC)

century and in 1699 a total of 28 Bideford ships went to the fishing grounds. The trade died away in the eighteenth century, but was revived in the nineteenth, and a few vessels even sailed over the bar to Newfoundland in the early-twentieth century. Ships would leave Bideford in February or March each year with salt and provisions; '... pork, flour, butter and a quantity of brandy, without which there is no living there.' There was something of a race to arrive, as the first captain had the right to settle quarrels as 'President of the bench'. Sailors felled trees and dragged them to the shore, where carpenters built 'stages' and small boats from which crews of three fished for cod with rod and line. They brought the fish ashore to splitters, headers, throat cutters, salters and barrow men. As well as directly employing some of Bideford's growing population, the fisheries provided work for shipbuilders, provision merchants and other traders. The valuable 'train' oil, processed from the cod, was brought home and shipped to Bristol and elsewhere. Much of the salt fish was taken direct to Mediterranean countries, which enabled the fishing vessels to crown a successful voyage by bringing oranges and lemons, nuts, figs, 'great raisins' and wine back to Bideford in time for Christmas.

Merchants and seamen making good profits from the Newfoundland trade were unwilling to send ships to serve the Queen. In 1591, when Bideford and Barnstaple were ordered to provide one ship of 100 tons, they replied that, of the only three large enough, two were in Newfoundland, and the other privateering. Three years earlier, however, when the Spanish Armada threatened, Adam Wyatt recorded that 'five ships went over the bar to join Sir F D at Plymo.' These were probably the vessels Grenville had fitted out for Virginia, the *Galleon Dudley* (250 tons), the *Virgin, God Save Her* (200 tons), the *Tiger*, the *St Leger*, and perhaps a vessel called *Golden Hind* (but not Drake's famous ship). He obeyed the Royal summons, and thus Bideford seamen played their part against the Armada. After this Grenville again tried to set up a plantation in Ireland, using Bideford as his port of embarkation and no doubt as a source of settlers.

In 1591, Grenville was again called on to serve the Queen, given command of the *Revenge*, and appointed vice-admiral of a squadron under Lord Thomas Howard, waiting for Spanish treasure ships returning from the Indies. After long delays there was fever among the men and the English ships were at 'Flores in the Azores' with the sick ashore, when a large Spanish fleet, including 20 warships, surprised them. Howard and the rest were able to 'catch the wind' and flee...

> But Sir Richard bore in hand all his sick men from the land
> Very carefully and slow,

> Men of Bideford in Devon,
> And we laid them on the ballast down below...

> And the little Revenge ran on sheer into the heart of the foe,
> With her hundred fighters on deck and her ninety sick below...

Tennyson's epic poem tells at length the story of 'the one and the fifty three', but Adam Wyatt tersely summed up in his diary the news that reached North Devon five weeks after the battle '... her Majesty's ship at sea, Sr Richard Greynfild Captaine, was taken by the Spaniards after encountering the whole Spanish Fleet for 2 daies.' Raleigh, after speaking to survivors, told how Grenville 'utterly refused to turne from the enemie'. When, mortally wounded, he asked his men to sink the ship, the few who were left refused and bargained with the Spaniards for their lives. Thus 'old Sir Richard, caught at last' was taken aboard the Spanish flagship and, dying there, set the seal on his reputation. His reported last words sum up the heroic aspects of his character:

> *Here die I, Richard Grenville, with a joyful and quiet mind, for that I have ended my life as a true soldier ought to do, that hath fought for his country, his Queen, religion, and honour; my soul willingly departing from out of this body, leaving behind the everlasting fame of a valiant soldier, having behaved as any is in duty bound to do.*

A man of his times, Grenville would probably be condemned nowadays as cruel and avaricious. One of his contemporaries complained bitterly of his 'intolerable pride and insatiable ambition', but his reckless daring and considerable success inspired 'men of Bideford in Devon' to follow him in search of profit or adventure – or both. He played a leading part in awakening the little town on the Torridge to a new world.

Two of the eight so-called 'Armada' cannons, which are in Victoria Park at the time of writing, after being used for many years as mooring posts on the Quay. Guns were often captured from enemy ships but there is no evidence that these came from the Spanish Armada. (PC)

This part of the Quay was added in the eighteenth century. This photograph shows what are the offices of Peter, Peter & Wright at the time of writing, and the adjoining shops before the shop fronts were inserted. (LM)

Right: *The old Bideford Harbour Office in King Street, c.1890. The banner over the door possibly refers to a mariners' insurance society or similar.* (BL)

Below: *Up until the seventeenth century these buildings sat almost directly next to the river. Over the centuries the Quay has been built out, and up, hence the 'sunken' doorway in The Old Ship Tavern.* (LM)

Left: *Bridgeland Street in quieter days. The magnificent building in the centre bears the dates 1692 and 1693 on its ornamental drainpipes and was built by Nathaniel Gascoyne.* (PC)

Chapter 4

Private Enterprise

Bideford's expansion in the century after the death of Sir Richard Grenville is symbolised by the magnificent merchants' houses of Bridgeland Street, built soon after 1690. It had already begun to be a thriving port and after a tussle with Barnstaple, which had always claimed the lead, its limits had been laid down as follows:

The Extent and Limits of the Port of Bideford Settled in the year 1676 – that is to say – From the farthest part West on the North side of the County of Devon in the parish of Wellcombe, and from thence Eastward to Hartland Point and Creek to Clovelly Quay; and from thenceon the sea coast as far as the port of Barnstaple, on the South side thereof. Also from a rock in the parish of Northam called Whipplestone or Hubba's Stone [the Hubbastone counted as Northam parish in those days] *in the West side of the River of Bideford, and from the pill called Jewell's Pill in the parish of Instow near the New Quay on the East side of the said River (to the south of the main part of Instow, and its Quay); and so on both sides of the river as far as the long Bridge of Bideford.*

This meant that Bideford could control all the creeks and sub-ports mentioned. Notice, however, that neither Instow nor Appledore was included that time but, according to a note made by a later customs officer:

Since writing the above, the Creek of Appledore has been added to the Port of Bideford – i.e. from the Barr to the Rock called Hubba's Stone; this was done in the Year 1813.

It took long enough to get, but this finally satisfied the traders of both places. Another note was also made, probably at the same time:

The Lawful Quay of Bideford is 428 feet in Length, extending from the stairs in the corner of Mr Heard's house to the Corner of Mr Banbury's house near Conduit Lane.

In the 100 years after 1676, progress was erratic, and eventually most of Bideford's overseas trade was captured by larger ports. Thus, by 1800, Bideford was only 'a small seaport town in a remote situation'

and by 1900 it had declined even further. This chapter traces its rise and part of its fall. Much of its rise was due to enterprise in the New World.

Among the most enterprising early-seventeenth-century merchants was George Shurt, a descendant of the Andrew family, and John Strange. They were owners or part-owners of a number of ships, and respectively employed the 60-ton *Zenobia* of Bideford and the *Barke Strange* in the Newfoundland fishery, which was attracting an increasing number of local vessels. The expansion of this fishery was among the main reasons for the rise of the port of Bideford.

Almost every merchant who could afford it had shares in a boat or in an 'adventure' to Newfoundland. For example, one merchant, Richard Sherman, whose will of 1643 is discussed later, had:

... a third part of the good ship or vessel named the Seaflower *of Bideford, of the burthen of three score* [60] *tons or there-abouts, now imployed at the New Found land in a fishing voyage and also the third part of all cables, anchors, sails, masts, yards, wragging* [rigging]*, tack-ling, furniture and apparel to the said ship belonging, with the appurtenances...*

At 60 tons the *Seaflower* would have been one of the larger vessels in the Newfoundland trade at that time.

When war with Spain ended in 1604, Shurt and Strange resumed and extended the export of cloth, bringing back cargoes of Spanish iron from Bilbao or San Sebastian, or wine and sugar from Spain and the Azores. Both sent out privateers in the wars with Spain and France in the late 1620s, but the part they played in establishing links with North America was of greater significance. John Strange was one of the few North Devon members of the London Virginia Company, while George Shurt and his brother Abraham established trade with New England.

Abraham Shurt, acting as agent for two wealthy Bristol merchants, had by 1629 founded a settlement at Pemaquid in northern Maine. This opened up trading opportunities for his family, and in 1630 George Shurt

Centre: *The memorial in St Mary's Church to John Strange, the heroic townsman who led efforts to stop the plague in the town, but who probably died from the disease himself in July 1646.* (BL)

Left: *The crowded waters of the Torridge in the heyday of colonial trade, as envisaged by Mark Myers, a noted local painter of maritime scenes.*

Right: *A fine view of the old cottages in North Road, c.1950. Formerly used by potters, several were demolished in the post-war clearances but some still survive into the twenty-first century. North Road, under its old name of Potters Lane, was once the only entrance into Bideford from Northam.* (PC)

Left: *Chudleigh Fort, East-the-Water, seen around the beginning of the twentieth century. This Civil War fort once controlled shipping and access to the bridge.* (LM)

Right: *Sailing vessels tied up against the wharves at East-the-Water in 1897. The Devon Trading Company's buildings have since gone and at the time of writing the site's future is under discussion.* (RC)

For many years this seventeenth-century merchant's house on the Quay was known as the 'Rose of Torridge' – its name borrowed from Kingsley's Westward Ho!. (PC)

sent the 80-ton *Friendship* of Bideford to Virginia, which at this time often meant all North America which belonged to England. Her cargo of blankets was probably destined for Pemaquid, for winters were hard and long on the coast of New England. A passenger on board the *Fellowship* off 'Nantasket', in October 1629, described 'our deck in the morning oer-spread with hoarie frost and dangling Isickles hung upon the Ropes'. This 170-ton vessel was returning home under her master George Luxon 'of Bittiford in Devonshire'. Transatlantic voyages were fraught with danger, and a few days later:

> *... the Mariners observed the rising of a little black cloud in the N.W. which increasing apace, made them prepare against a coming storm, the wind in short time grew to boisterous bringing after us a huge grown Sea, at five of the clock it was pitchie dark... the storm augmenting still... we lost our rudder and with that our hopes... all the while we saw many dead bodies of men and women floating by us.*

Fortunately the damage was repaired, and after a 40-day voyage the *Fellowship* 'arrived before Bittiford'.

John Strange died in 1646, Bideford's plague year. This, and the Civil War which preceded it, set back economic progress, and Bideford did not recover until after the return of Charles II to the throne in 1660. George Shurt, who died in 1658, left his brother Abraham a new house on the Quay, 'God sending him home to live in Bideford'. However, Abraham Shurt stayed in Pemaquid, where another member of the family, Adam Shurt, was town clerk in the 1680s. Such agents took relations and servants with them and became a focus for settlement as well as for trade. Emigration to New England continued throughout the century and, soon after 1700, a settlement on the coast of Maine was named Biddeford.

The seventeenth century also saw an increase in voyages made by small ships, whose masters often marketed their own cargoes, particularly Bideford pottery. The expanding pottery manufacture stimulated other industry and trade. Welsh miners were employed to exploit the local seam of culm (anthracite), probably to provide some of the fuel needed for kilns. Bideford's parish registers show 'A welchman a Collier' buried in 1629, while entries such as 'John Boorges, Collier, founde deade in the Culme worke' in 1655 illustrate the dangers of mining. The main Bideford pit, which was in the rectory grounds, and gave Pitt Lane its name, was waterlogged by 1680, so fuel was then shipped from Wales. The small ships that brought it took back butter pots, milk pans and pitchers for the Welsh dairying industry. Ireland needed even more pottery and in one year, 1683, over 140,000 parcels of Bideford earthenware were shipped there at the height of a 'butter boom', which created a demand for pots in which to export it. This large-scale trade was exploited by merchants with Irish connections, and the fortunes of some of Bideford's leading commercial families then owed as much to local pots and Irish butter as to the famous Virginia tobacco trade.

A westerly position was an advantage for transatlantic trade, and merchants, mariners and settlers from Bideford were among the first to exploit it. Some tobacco was imported before the Civil War and, after the Restoration, Bideford built up a fleet of tobacco ships, with names like *Virginia Merchant*, *Adventure*, and *Merchants' Delight*. In 1676 one vessel alone, the *Bideford Merchant*, brought 135,000lbs of tobacco from Maryland for a new generation of merchants – Abraham Heiman, Anthony Hopkins and, the most respected, John Davie, who used the profits of colonial trade to build a great house (part of what is, at the time of writing, the Royal Hotel). Bideford's commercial success drew in merchants from outside, who helped to extend the town's mercantile base and establish it as a leading tobacco

Another of Mark Myers' immensely atmospheric paintings, this one is entitled 'The Return of the Dove' and shows the Dove *of Bideford, off Lundy, limping home under jury-rig, after being dismasted in a violent storm in mid-Atlantic.*

port. By 1690 they included Antoine Juliot, a French Huguenot, and the Irishmen Thomas Power, Hartwell Buck and John Smith.

A nonconformist, John Smith was banned by the Corporation Act of 1661 from taking part in local government, so never became mayor, although he was one of the richest merchants. He traded with Waterford and Ross, where his father and brother provisioned ships for the colonies. Another brother owned a plantation in Virginia, while yet another was a ship's master in the colonial trade. He had a number of vessels built in the colonies, where timber was abundant and the waterways less crowded than the Torridge. The largest was the 200-ton *Factor*, built on the Chester River in Maryland in 1696. Smith and other merchants made Bideford important as an entrepôt, shipping out tobacco to European and Irish ports, and bringing back goods for re-export. Employment was also boosted by the export of locally-produced items. The first cargo shipped to Maryland by John Smith in the *Factor* was a large and varied one. It consisted of woollen cloth – Barnstaple bays, fustians, worsteds and serges; linen from Germany and Ireland; some lawn and a little thrown silk; 5lbs of wick-yarn; rugs, curtain material, blankets and three bedticks; woollen wearing apparel, a dozen neckcloths, four hundredweight of haberdashery, six dozen handkerchiefs; 497lbs of shoes, 25 dozen stockings, 16 dozen felt hats, 48 pairs of bodices; 13 saddles, six horsecollars; a chest of drawers, 18 rush seat chairs; 5lbs of lead shot, 70lbs of pewter, 20 hundredweight of cast-iron wares, 20lbs of nails, two dozen sieves; three reams of paper, 20lbs of spicery and eight barrels of strong beer – all shipped from Bideford Quay in the seventeenth century and all welcomed by people setting up home far away.

As sole owner of vessels and their cargoes, Smith took great risks and, in 1700, claimed to have lost £3,000 when the *Pearl* of Bideford was seized by pirates off Newfoundland. Bideford merchants had a lot to lose when wars with France in 1689–97 and 1702–13 disrupted shipping and trade in general, virtually cut off European markets, and caused heavy losses in the Newfoundland fleet. They also seriously affected the tobacco trade – one lost cargo was valued at £1,500. The eighteenth century therefore started inauspiciously for many of Bideford's traders and, in 1706, 'John Smith, a great dealer to the plantations and other parts... having met with many great losses and misfortunes... died in debt upwards of £10,000.'

In 1715, John Fontaine, a young Huguenot, described the people of Bideford as 'the most ungenteel, niggardly and inbred that ever I see, most of the inhabitants being sailors.' He had joined the *Dove* of Bideford in Ireland as a passenger to Virginia, but a great storm in mid-Atlantic had forced the vessel home for repairs, and Fontaine, disgruntled at having to wait for another passage, did not care for Bideford. After a successful second voyage, however, he was pleased enough to follow up contacts given him by the town's Virginia merchants. George Buck, son of the Irish merchant, Hartwell Buck, the most important of these, made use of his brother and son (both called John) as his agents in the colonies, where they purchased plantations and had ships built, thus controlling all aspects of the family business and building up the Bideford tobacco trade to new heights over the next 30 years. In the ten-year period 1722–31, for example, customs records show 8,450,427lbs of tobacco were brought into Bideford, mainly for re-export to Europe. Much tobacco was also brought in to Instow, which was part of the port of Barnstaple, by Bideford merchants who did so in the hope of avoiding customs checks. It was obviously listed by Barnstaple, so the Bideford tobacco trade was larger than the records show – especially if the Bideford merchants got away without recording it at all, which was more usual than it should have been! After 1740, however, another war with France

This extract from an eighteenth-century sketch map of Bideford, possibly drawn by one of the Donn family, shows that the customs house (at the top of the picture) was then in Bridge Street. (NDRO)

forced tobacco ships to sail round the north of Ireland to Liverpool or Whitehaven, to avoid lurking privateers. George Buck, abandoning nonconformity, had been Mayor of Bideford no fewer than six times: he died in 1743, and his son John followed in 1745. Their successors preferred the life of landed gentry, and the remaining merchants were neither rich nor numerous enough to engage in large-scale trade. The war ended in 1748, but Bideford, lacking the facilities of larger ports, did not recover its former pre-eminence.

Fortunately for the town, other traders also played a part in its economy. In the seventeenth century merchants like Joseph Comer and Richard Greening traded with Ireland, and by doing so added quite a bit of prosperity to the town. Comer carried all sorts of cargo, but usually took pottery to Dublin, and he exported over 3,000 dozen pieces of pottery in 11 years after 1664. He appears to have taken his last cargo there in 1699 and, when there was war or rebellion, shipped troops for the government. His will shows that he had a 'shopp of goods' worth £300, a great deal in those days, and he owned two houses, about £1,500 in money, and a quarter share in a vessel, the *Swan*, which was a 'pink' (a sailing ship with a narrow stern). Richard Greening who also traded with Dublin was equally prosperous leaving £1,000 in money, two houses and land, as well as his shipping. He was lost at sea in 1686. In the eighteenth century there were still quite a number of smaller traders who, for example, sent small ships to Liverpool and Warrington, for rock salt, which was boiled down in seawater to make 'salt on salt' to preserve the local catch of herrings.

Limestone was also brought by sea, together with culm to burn it for use on the land. An agricultural writer of the 1790s observed:

On the shore of the estuary, opposite to the town, are several limekilns, now in full work. Numbers of pack-horses, and a few carts, loading, or waiting for loads.

Bideford Quay c.1880 – before there were any trees present. The small scale of the loads carried by the ships can be seen by the pile of goods in the bottom left-hand corner of the photograph. The absence of any traffic is astonishing to a modern car driver. (AB)

The customs house at the bottom of Bridgeland Street replaced the one in Bridge Street. Since this 1985 photograph was taken the building has gone through a number of name changes. (PC)

The stone, chiefly, and the culm with which it is burnt, wholly brought across the channel from the coast of Wales...

Lime had been burnt at Bideford at least since the sixteenth century, and there were now new kilns at East-the-Water, built by George Heard, a cooper, probably with the help of a mortgage from a fellow townsman. In the days before reliable banking, ships' shares were also popular with people seeking outlets for spare capital. Shareholders did not have to be in a maritime trade; Peter Glubb, an attorney, had shares in two vessels, one of which was the *Dove*, so nearly lost in mid-Atlantic with the young

One of the many limekilns found around the area. This one exists in 2004 on the Tarka Trail and is a poignant reminder of this once-flourishing industry. (LM)

The Rope Walk, with its sheds alongside. The buildings have gone, but at the time of writing the long narrow lane remains as a reminder of one of the town's maritime industries.

Huguenot John Fontaine on-board. Glubb sold his one-eighth share for £35.2s.6d. in 1726, by which time the vessel, built in Virginia for the Smith family in 1699, had probably repaid her shareholders. Multiple ownership helped the growth of ports and shipping and, by spreading risks, encouraged small shareholders. Apart from four sixty-fourths held by a gentleman from an adjoining parish, the *Star*, a Bideford vessel built in the early-nineteenth century, was owned in the town – by her builder, her master, a sailmaker, a twine spinner, a scrivener, two drapers, an ironmonger, a painter, a coal merchant, a blacksmith, and two merchants.

One of the merchants holding shares in the *Star* was Robert Wren, a member of the family that owned the ropewalk behind Bridgeland Street, which it predated. It was the centre of a thriving industry with 'the Yarnehouse, the Tarrehouse, and Hatchell house [where hemp was combed]... and Lofts, Shopps and Chambers to the same belonging.' Another ropewalk at East-the-Water went out of production before the mid-eighteenth century, but the Wrens' business flourished and in the 1780s, Josias, the head of the firm, had shares in several ships. Some vessels were owned exclusively by the Wren family – the 84-ton brigantine, *Bideford*, for example, built at Portsmouth, New Hampshire in 1749. In 1767 they had the 140-ton *Sally*, built beside the same river, the Piscataqua, where settlers from Bideford and district had first built ships to send home over 100 years before. Robert Wren, a master-mariner, kept an account book which showed that the *Sally* cost just over £1,200. Used at first in the Newfoundland trade, she later made voyages to Holland and the Baltic, and was also used in the coastal trade. She earned her owners about £800 before she was sold for £803 in 1779. By then there was little profit in shipping, due to the American Revolutionary War, which also involved France, Spain and Holland. After the loss of the colonies, Bideford ships could not so easily be built in New England, so the Wrens' new 166-ton brigantine, *Albion*, was launched into the Torridge at Bideford.

The trading communities of small ports in the eighteenth century were vulnerable in wartime. Bideford's shipping had scarcely recovered from the previous conflict when, in 1793, war began with revolutionary France, and continued until the end of the century.

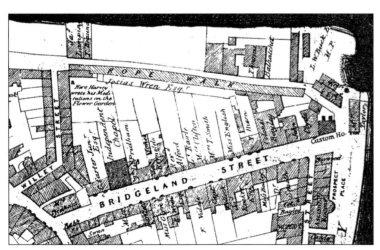

Above: *The Rope Walk, shown clearly on this 1842 map, was where ropes were made, and was owned for many years by the Wren family.* (PC)

Above right: *A milestone from North America brought home by an early traveller. It can be found in a garden in Bridgeland Street at the time of writing.* (PC)

Chapter 5

The Shipbuilders

By 1800, although Bideford's seaborne trade had contracted, the port still had potential. In the nineteenth century, after making a small contribution to the defeat of Napoleon, and riding out the post-war depression, Bideford enjoyed a shipping boom before economic and industrial change brought the old maritime order to an end.

The war with France which, with one short inter-mission, lasted until 1815, brought both problems and opportunities. Overseas trade, long in decline, now virtually disappeared, as prudent owners and managers withdrew their ships from long risky voyages. Robert Wren, for example, took the *Albion* out of the Newfoundland trade and employed her coastally. Later, however, she was one of the local vessels under contract to the government to carry supplies for Wellington's army fighting in Spain and Portugal, with profit and risk nicely balanced. Her 11 voyages to Lisbon between 1809 and 1814 earned £440 a year on average, compared with £200 in peace-time, but inflation had reduced the value of money. After 1810, with insurance premiums consuming over 30 per cent of dividends, it appears that the *Albion*'s owners decided not to insure their elderly vessel. The gamble paid off until 1815. Presumably carrying supplies for the troops that fought at Waterloo, she was lost off Ostend that summer, 30 years after her launch.

Government work was also welcomed by Bideford shipbuilders. A total of 15 small warships were built on the Torridge between 1806 and 1815, five of them in William Taylor's yard at Cross Park, East-the-Water. This was opposite the aptly named Ship on Launch inn now used by a firm of financial advisers. The 427-ton, 16-gun sloop of war, *Comet*, built in 1807, was in action the next year, when she captured the *Sylphe*, an 18-gun French vessel, off the coast of Spain. Taylor built two more sloops, the *Carnation* (1807) and the *Fairy* (1812), as well as the more aggressively named *Mastiff*, a 182-ton gunboat, and *Beelzebub*, a bomb ship of 325 tons, both launched in 1813. Admiralty contracts did not solve all wartime problems for, according to a letter written in 1810 by Richard Chapman, a leading shipbuilder, there were ten shipyards on the Taw and Torridge, but 'two of the Yards could have performed all the work for three Years past, [and] at this time there is not work bespoke for one yard.' Chapman built warships at Upper Cleave Houses (Bank End), then in Northam parish, but George Crocker worked in Bideford, where he built the *Acorn*, a 26-gun sloop of

war in 1807. Crocker had 'premises behind the Rope Path in Bideford... as far as the low water mark on the north part thereof.' This yard therefore faced the Pill, but Crocker probably had access to the old yard below Bridgeland Street, from which he launched a 430-ton warship into the Torridge. The project seems to have rather strained his finances: in 1808 he went bankrupt, with the lease of his yard being acquired by Thomas Burnard.

Burnard, a timber merchant and shipowner, had problems of his own for, when Napoleon extended his blockade after the Treaty of Tilsit with Russia in 1807, England had great difficulty in obtaining Baltic timber. For over 200 years cargoes of Norway deals, red Riga pine, 'great masts' and 'small masts' had been brought to Bideford, at first by Norwegian and Dutch vessels, and then by ships owned in the port. The shipbuilders and seaborne trade of Bideford and all other ports were under serious threat unless another source of suitable timber could be found to provide planking, masts and spars, for the building and repair of wooden ships. The forests of North America provided the answer, and the arrival in Bideford of the ship *Ann* at the end of 1810, with lumber from St Andrews, New Brunswick, heralded the revival of the port's transatlantic trade.

Like many Bideford merchants before him, Thomas Burnard sought a colonial trading and ship-building base. Taking advantage of the protection afforded Canadian trade by continuing high tariffs on Baltic timber, he sent out a master shipwright, William Ellis, and two apprentices to Prince Edward Island in 1818. Again following precedent, he sent a member of his family – his nephew, Thomas Burnard Chanter – to act as his agent. In 1820, the *Mars* (342 tons), the first vessel to be built for Burnard in Prince Edward Island, was registered in Bideford, and was quickly followed by the 89-ton *Lavinia*, and in 1821 by the *Bacchus* (234 tons), and the *Apollo* (141 tons). All brought back cargoes of timber and Burnard began to use the two larger vessels in regular trade with the island. There a settlement called New Bideford grew, and people from old Bideford began to emigrate there. Thomas Burnard died in 1823 and the *Mars* was lost the following year, but by then the connection with Prince Edward Island was firmly established. The health of the local fleet is shown from a govern-ment survey of 1819 which recorded 110 vessels registered in the port of Bideford.

In 1824 Lord Rolle began constructing a canal between Torrington and Weare Giffard where it

Above: *This painting shows the* Sedwell Jane, *a three-masted schooner built at the Rolle Canal Company's shipyard at Sea Lock, two miles above Bideford bridge in 1868. The reversed name on the flag is an artistic conceit.* (PC)

Left: *A packed scene in Barnstaple Street, c.1900, looking towards the Royal Hotel. Note the horse dung in the street; this picture was taken before cars came into common usage.* (BL)

Right: *An early-nineteenth-century sketch by Thomas Rowlandson of the River Torridge below Bideford.*

Below: *The schooner* Pride of the Torridge *painted at Palermo in Sicily. She was built at Waters' yard, East-the-Water, in 1858.* (NDMT)

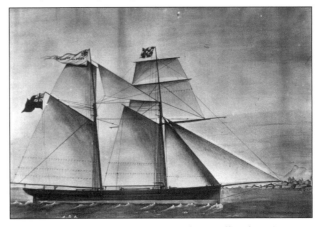

Above: *The connection between emigration and the timber trade can be clearly seen in Richard Heard's advertisement in the* North Devon Journal *from 1850.* (NDJ)

linked up with the River Torridge. At the latter place a small shipyard began work around 1827 producing small coasters, many of which seem to have had their final fitting out in one of the better-equipped Bideford yards. The manager of the canal eventually went bankrupt in 1865 and the canal was sold to the railway company who used much of its course for their trackway.

By 1830, Thomas Burnard Chanter had returned to Bideford, where he was a:

considerable shipowner... and in the early days of emigration sent many ships from Bideford to British colonies in North America, and the USA, bringing back timber and other produce.

For various reasons, mainly economic, there was a growing desire to emigrate at that time, providing opportunities for Bideford shipowners. In 1850 a Devon directory recorded:

Four first-class emigrant ships (belonging to Mr. Richard Heard) sail from Bideford to America etc. Passengers find this a very desirable port to start from for the western shores; and it is remarkable that no accident has happened to any of the ships which have left Bideford with emigrants during the last twenty years.

Richard Heard, who lived at East-the-Water, was originally a builder, and it is said that he used his wife's money to build what is now Grenville Street, then called Emma Street in her honour. He sent one of his sons as his agent to Prince Edward Island, to supervise supplies of timber and the building of his emigrant ships, the first of which was the *Em B. Heard*. She arrived in Bideford in 1841 and was followed the next year by the *Civility*.

An emigrant on the *Civility* kept a diary, which he afterwards sent home. The little leather-covered book, with its faded brown ink, conveys a vivid picture of the voyage of the writer, William Fulford, a Methodist lay preacher from nearby Buckland Brewer who, with family and friends, embarked at Bideford Quay in April 1848. On leaving, the *Civility* lay overnight at Appledore, then:

... Mr Herd came on Board and gave Order to the Captain to go over the Bar... and we were Piloted Over the Bar to Encounter the Boisterousness of the Winds and Waves of the Attalantic Ocean. And through the Sailing and Rowling of the Vessel we and all the Passengers were Seasick throughout the Day.

All recovered a few days later, and became hungry. Fulford found 'sea biskit with so much horse bean flour in it... serves to produce indigestion,' but emigrants could buy bread 'for a penny pr loaf also a Pie or Pudden at one halfpenny, as there is an excellent Coock.' They also had:

Baken or Ham dry or in pickel, Salt Herrings or large fish, Rice, dry peas, potatoes, good Sweed Turnips and Sallery [celery], lump Sugar, treacle, Currants, Thoney [honey], Currant jillee [jelly], Pickled Onions, Coffe, Coko, peperments... also Chees... Appels, [and] Medicine viz Antibilious Pills, best Epsom Salts and Senna.

Ford Yard below Devonshire Park, c.1985. It has now been demolished and awaits redevelopment at the time of writing. (PC)

Below: *Looking back towards the shipyards on the riverside at East-the-Water in the mid-nineteenth century. The small white building to the upper left is the entrance to the 'Bideford Black' mine.* (PC)

Left: *Two vessels on the stocks at Johnson's yard near the bridge, c.1870. Note the rather haphazard form of scaffolding around the ships.*

Below: *Another view of the East-the-Water shipyards with three ships on the stocks and one finished vessel in the water.* (PC)

Passengers could buy 'French brandy, gin and Rum, good Cider and Vinegar,' but if they wanted water they were forced to flavour it with peppermint for, as Fulford wrote when a cask was opened one morning, it 'stinked aloud'!

William Fulford wrote in detail about everything he saw, including 'a whale about two thirds the length of our vessel.' There were days with 'the Sun and Sky bright and clear and Verry pleasant on the top Deck' and nights when 'torrents of rain and sea pour'd down the Hatchways into the hold.' It was overcrowded down there.

We are so Closely Situated [sic] *in our Births and our Breath Contracts so much impure Air and the Nausiousness of our Chamber Slops tis almost enought to create the plague...*

To pass the time profitably, Fulford often got together the 14 children on board and 'teached them to Read and Spel'! The climax of the voyage came when the Banks of Newfoundland were crossed, and Father Neptune came aboard, with traditional ceremony. Then the *Civility* entered the St Lawrence, and at Quebec one great adventure ended and another began for the 51 emigrants she had carried from Bideford.

By the 1850s the Newfoundland trade had revived, and there was also some trade with Mediterranean countries. Transatlantic voyages with emigrants out and timber back continued, and numerous ships were built in Prince Edward Island for Bideford owners. An enterprising Bideford shoemaker opened up an export market in Australia, for boots and shoes for emigrants to the goldfields, and later the *Surprise* of Bideford, only 49 tons, lived up to her name by sailing to New Zealand. She was built by Robert Johnson at East-the-Water in 1847. On the other side of the river, the Upper Cleave Houses yard was flourishing under John Evans and George Cox but, in the 1850s, when full-rigged 'clipper' ships were being built there, the town boundary had not been extended to include this yard. Thus the *Sarah Neuman*, 1,004 tons, the largest vessel launched into the Torridge in the nineteenth century, was not in fact built in Bideford. George Crocker, who

Chapter 6

Road, River and Rail

The history of transport in and around Bideford has been one of constant change, as routes and types of traffic have come and gone over the centuries. The original ford not only gave the town its name, but marked the first route through it. From the west, the track must have descended the ridge from Handy Cross, behind the site of Westcroft School, to the river where Ford House now stands. The ford was presumably a bank of pebbles or hard sand shallow enough to cross at low tide. Early writers have spoken of a paved roadway running down to the river but, if it ever existed, the evidence has been lost. On the east side, the traveller probably followed the line of the old Barnstaple Road towards Eastleigh, or of Torrington Street up to Torrington Lane and out to Gammaton, where in later years a public house stood to refresh travellers.

The old roads to Barnstaple and Torrington continued in use after the bridge had been built, and the ford abandoned, but Bridge Street and High Street became the new main routes, leading by way of Old Town to Handy Cross. Entrance into the town itself was via Allhalland Street, for then only river silt and private gardens lay between the bridge and the end of the Quay at Conduit Lane. In 1439 a second road reached the town, when a causeway (twenty-first-century Northam Road) was built across the marshes of the Kenwith Valley. This later linked up with the ferry service to Braunton, as shown on a seventeenth-century map. By this time transport was improving, and goods could be consigned to regular carriers who, with their strings of packhorses, often

Horses were a vital part of the transport system before the development of cars, and here we see a fine array of horses for sale outside the Pannier Market just before the First World War. (BL)

Northam Road marks the route of the old causeway linking Northam to Bideford. Here the site of today's Post Office has just been prepared so that building could begin, sometime in the 1930s. (BL)

formed large parties, which travellers joined for safety. In 1680, for example, a man left London on a Monday, probably by regular passenger coach to Exeter, 'from whence he came with the Carryer unto the Towne of Great Torrington and from thence... he came unto this town [Bideford] upon Saturday.' It was notoriously difficult for wheeled traffic to penetrate North Devon's 'bushie lanes'. Local gentry, who had their coaches made high 'on purpose for these roads', then found they had to pay to take their vehicles across Bideford bridge. In 1714 the toll for a coach was 5s., and for a 'charriott' 2s.6d.

Tolls became more general as local roads were turnpiked, the first being the (old) Barnstaple–Bideford road in 1763. Improvements were slow, however, and packhorses were still carrying goods inland in the 1790s. There appears to have been a coach to Exeter then, which must have given its passengers a good jolting, for the road to Torrington was as yet unimproved. An early coach service was begun by a Mr Garrett and sold by his widow in 1804 to J. Dorman. In 1827 the coach crashed as it was entering Bideford along Torrington Lane, but no one was killed on this occasion, although fatal accidents did happen. A directory of 1830 listed two passenger coaches which ran three times weekly – the *Torridge Express* to Exeter and the *North Devon*, which connected Barnstaple and Plymouth via Bideford. There were also 14 carriers' wagons, presumably including George Pugsley's 'fly waggon', advertised in 1829 to run to Barnstaple four days a week.

Left: A striking photograph, c.1880, of what is now Natwest Bank. The bollards and chains to the right were to stop carriages in High Street plunging into the river. (PC)

Right: A very leisurely mode of transport in the 1925 Pageant! Records exist of the use of sedan chairs in the area. (RLK)

Below: A view of holidaymakers as they set out from the New Inn at around the turn of the nineteenth century. (SO)

Above: *Pridham & Son were a famous family of local carters, and here their 'Pantechnicon' vehicle is seen outside their office near Jubilee Square, c.1900.*

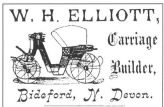

Right: *Advertisements from c.1910 showing the horse-drawn removal van used by a local firm.* (PC)

W. H. ELLIOTT,
Carriage Builder,
Bideford, N. Devon.

Carriages of Every Description Built to Order on
the Newest and Most Improved Principles.
New and Second-Hand Carriages always in Stock.

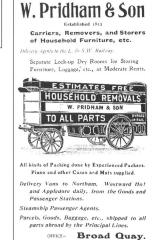

W. Pridham & Son
Established 1812
**Carriers, Removers, and Storers
of Household Furniture, etc.**

Delivery Agents to the L. & S.W. Railway.

Separate Lock-up Dry Rooms for Storing
Furniture, Luggage, etc., at Moderate Rents.

ESTIMATES FREE
HOUSEHOLD REMOVALS
W. PRIDHAM & SON
TO ALL PARTS

All kinds of Packing done by Experienced Packers.
Piano and other Cases and Mats supplied.

*Delivery Vans to Northam, Westward Ho!
and Appledore daily, from the Goods and
Passenger Stations.*

Steamship Passenger Agents.

*Parcels, Goods, Baggage, etc., shipped to all
parts abroad by the Principal Lines.*

OFFICE— **Broad Quay.**

Above: *Bideford Turnpike Trust's toll-house at the top of Clovelly Road. Sold off when the Trust closed in the 1880s, it became a private house and later a shop (Twinaways). At the time of writing it is a house once again.* (PC)

Right: *This handsome four-horse carriage, photographed c.1890, would have been used to carry visitors to Westward Ho! on day-trips and similar outings.*

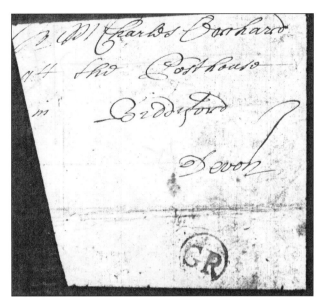

This letter, sent to a local gentleman in 1684, shows that Bideford had a post house even then. (WP)

Amid this flurry of development, pedestrians were not forgotten – in January 1825, tenders were invited for the embanking of the marsh north of the Pill. The work created the area that later became Victoria Park, and provided a footpath to Northam. In 1844 a bridge was built across the Pill to link this path with the Quay and, although it embarrassingly collapsed just before being opened, it created a direct route to Northam. The Pill was covered in at the end of the nineteenth century to allow the Bideford, Westward Ho! and Appledore Railway to be built, and in 1927 Kingsley Road replaced the 500-year-old causeway.

The new turnpike road from Torrington, begun in 1825, hugged the west side of the Torridge, necessitating large earthworks. When it reached Bideford, instead of continuing along the riverbank and ending at the bridge, it was unexpectedly carried up Torridge Hill, which was specially built to take it. This odd route was chosen for 'private reasons'– it was the hope of the owner of the New Inn opposite the Pannier Market that it would generate passing trade! The

townspeople, it is said, were so incensed that they got up a subscription and, after a benefit performance by a local amateur company, began constructing what is known as New Road. Unfortunately they ran out of money and the rival turnpikers took it over, placing their toll-house at the bottom of Torridge Hill, and leaving New Road as a cul-de-sac.

In 1829 the town's roads were 'macadamised', beginning with Mill Street and Allhalland Street. At the same time some old houses in Potters Lane (known as North Road at the time of writing) were removed to improve the entrance into the town from Northam. Three years later another turnpike road was built along the coastal plain to Barnstaple via Instow. This took nearly two years to build and cost £5,535, but quickly became the main link between the two towns. The toll-house stood at the junction of the old and new roads, tolls being charged until the 1870s, when the system came to an end. Returns, printed annually in the local paper over the years 1837–45, show that the receipts of the Bideford Turnpike Trust averaged £2,100 per annum, a large sum in those days.

By 1850 there was a twice-daily omnibus to Barnstaple, a daily coach to Exeter, and others to Plymouth, Hartland and Torrington. More places were served by carriers, with more services. In 1853, Bideford's leading coach firm, Pridham & Lake, began their New Royal Mail service to London. This, however, was the peak of the coaching age for, within two years, the arrival of the 'iron horse' in Bideford forced Pridham & Lake to sell off many of their live ones. By the 1860s there was only one omnibus running from the town, and even that disappeared within a decade.

In later years Tanton's Hotel was known as a posting house, as shown in this photograph, c.1900. (PC)

Road transport was slow in the early-nineteenth century. Note that passengers were also conveyed in this cumbersome horse wagon. The poster dates from c.1830. (PC)

A line of lighters moored just below the police station in the interwar period. They were a vital part of the local transport network – and, as our roads become ever more congested, may well make a comeback! (LM)

In 1864–66 the bridge was widened to nearly 24 feet; in 1925, it was increased to 30 feet at a cost of about £40,000, and the road at the western end was widened at the same time. As detailed in the chapter on the Bridge Trust, increasing traffic on the bridge led to the collapse and subsequent repair of two arches, but clearly a more lasting solution had to be found.

In 1982 a six-week public enquiry was held into the route for the Bideford bypass and, against strong local opposition, a site downstream was selected for a bridge from Westleigh to Northam, with the road continuing along a viaduct across the Kenwith Valley to rejoin the A39 at Abbotsham Cross. Notwithstanding poor weather and difficulties with the manufacture of supports, Torridge bridge opened on time in 1987 and altered the entire road pattern of Bideford. In 2004 a third bridge was also suggested to relieve continuing pressure on the old bridge.

Small craft carrying passengers and freight up and down the Torridge were such an everyday feature of Bideford life, that little was written about them until an account of 1755:

The boats used on the river for hire are passage boats, ballast boats and lighters; in the passage boats a passenger is carried from Bideford to Appledore three miles for a penny, and the hire of a lighter that will carry ten tons for a whole tide is five shillings.

A rare record of a 'passage' or ferry boat is found in a local newspaper report of a court case in 1873, fought by an Appledore mariner's wife who 'plied in a boat' between her home and Bideford, and was known as Captain Sally Smallridge. Other barges were used to carry goods to and from vessels moored downriver, and provided cheap transport for heavy loads such as clay, coal, bricks and agricultural produce. Some barges were propelled by long sweeps, but sailing barges, mainly used for the extraction of gravel from the estuary, were also operated by Bideford owners. Between tides, 40 tons of gravel would be shovelled aboard by two-man crews, who then had to shovel it all out again at Bideford. Between the wars the barges gradually became motorised but their number declined, being replaced by large modern suction-dredgers which now rarely discharge gravel at Bideford.

The first herald of a new age in water transport was the *Lady Rodney* steam packet which sailed up the Torridge in January 1827. She ran aground near the bridge, presumably to the delight of sailing-ship masters, who resented this newfangled competition, but the steamer's owners, making the best of a bad job, paid the town crier to announce conducted tours of the stranded ship at 6d. a head. At high tide she was floated off, to the cheers of a huge crowd. Later in the same year, a service was started between Bristol, Bideford and Barnstaple, but it only lasted a month, and it was six years before another effort was made, this time with the *Bristol* steam packet, a wooden paddle steamer 100 feet long. This service lasted just two months.

Within a few weeks of its demise, however, local merchants had set up a Bideford-based company and

Above: *Elliott's Garage in the 1950s, has since changed considerably over the years as the owners have kept up to date with motorists' requirements.* (AB)

Right: *The workshop area of Elliott's Garage in the 1930s.* (AB)

Below: *An interior view of Elliott's Garage in the 1930s showing a prospective customer trying out a new car.* (AB)

Above: *The* Devonia *at Bristol, c.1910, with passengers bound for Bideford.* (NDMT)

Right: *Passengers were conveyed in horse carriages all over the area, but in 1847 a Torrington-bound one went over the Quay. These verses from a broadsheet of the time describe the 'awful accident'.* (NDRO)

Below: *The* Iron Duke (left), *the* Devonia, *and another 'puffer' alongside, with a steam lorry on the Quay, c.1922.* (NDMT)

Reflect, dwell and ponder, fond hearts torn asunder,
   On the last quoted scene of dismay,
When an Omnibus full, by a horse out of rule,
   Was sunk with eight lives o'er the Quay.

JOHN CHAPPLE, kind-hearted, among the departed,
   His equal is not to be found ;
Was a friend to the poor, and many folks more,
   For his soul did with goodness abound.

Mothers FRIENDSHIP in water, with one little DAUGHTER,
   MRS. PAGE, too drown'd by their side,
BETTY GRIFFEY, ANN NORMAN, MR. PASSMORE, wool-forman,
   In this ill-fated coffin all died.

There were two survivors, good swimmers, tho' divers,
   Escaped from this terrible death ;
One Man through the door, and a woman before,
   Were the souls this sad story saith.

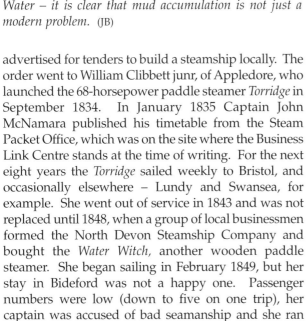

A very early photograph showing the wharves at East-the-Water – it is clear that mud accumulation is not just a modern problem. (JB)

The Privateer *of Swansea, a steam-paddle tug, used for summer excursions, was a familiar sight at Bideford in the 1890s.* (NDMT)

advertised for tenders to build a steamship locally. The order went to William Clibbett junr, of Appledore, who launched the 68-horsepower paddle steamer *Torridge* in September 1834. In January 1835 Captain John McNamara published his timetable from the Steam Packet Office, which was on the site where the Business Link Centre stands at the time of writing. For the next eight years the *Torridge* sailed weekly to Bristol, and occasionally elsewhere – Lundy and Swansea, for example. She went out of service in 1843 and was not replaced until 1848, when a group of local businessmen formed the North Devon Steamship Company and bought the *Water Witch,* another wooden paddle steamer. She began sailing in February 1849, but her stay in Bideford was not a happy one. Passenger numbers were low (down to five on one trip), her captain was accused of bad seamanship and she ran aground several times. She was sold in August 1851 and laid up at Bristol for four years. She only returned to the town in 1855, to be 'ignominiously' converted to a clipper schooner, but even this did not work out, and she was scrapped in 1863.

The *Princess Royal,* which was driven by a metal screw or propeller instead of a wooden paddle wheel and capable of carrying nearly 100 passengers and freight, replaced the *Water Witch* in January 1852. She made the run to Bristol for the next 19 years and was noted for her comfort and punctuality. The arrival of the railway in 1855, however, spelt the end of this brief period of glory. Most of the ships that served the port after the *Princess Royal* lasted only a short time and had to scratch around for cargoes. In 1881, for example, Thomas Wickham bought the *Marquis of Lorne,* an iron-built screw ship which ran until 1894. In that year, however, the *Devonia* was built for the Bideford and Bristol Steamship Company, managed by Edward Tattersill, a local grocer. Although she occasionally carried passengers, this trim little craft, a familiar sight on the Torridge in the early years of the

twentieth century, was used mainly for cargo, particularly gravel for the construction of new docks at Avonmouth, Portishead and in South Wales. For a time she served as the Lundy packet, in succession to the sailing cutter *Lundy Gannet.* That name was also used for a small diesel vessel, which served the island for many years after 1956. At the time of writing the larger *MV Oldenburg* takes goods and passengers to Lundy from Bideford, and pleasure steamers, once numerous on the Torridge, still occasionally visit Bideford in the summer months.

The railway came late to Bideford, even though a line to Okehampton was proposed as early as 1831. In 1845, during the railway boom, companies were formed to promote four lines – one to Tavistock, one to Tiverton, and two between Bideford and Exeter. The Town Council and local merchants favoured the first on grounds of cost, but one of the Bideford–Exeter links was accepted by Parliament. Owing to the collapse of the railway 'bubble', and a battle over the gauge of the track, the line linking Bideford to Barnstaple, and thus to Exeter, was not opened until 29 October 1855. Known as the Bideford Extension Railway, it cost £44,000 and was built by the contractor Thomas Brassey, his engineer W.R. Neale and an army of 'navvies'. On its opening day, the line carried some 4,000 people to the town, the first of many millions.

Until 1862 the line was leased by the contractors – the usual practice in those days – but in that year it became part of the London and South Western Railway. By then five trains a day were making the journey to Exeter, and both passenger and goods traffic were healthy. Further income was generated by special trains – to Torquay, Plymouth, Bristol and even London. The LSWR needed this income as they spent heavily on improving both the line and the rolling stock. In 1872, the company extended the line to Torrington, thus increasing Bideford's traffic. A new station was built behind the Royal Hotel, with a

Right: *Bideford station staff line up for their photograph, c.1920. Left to right, back row: Ernie Bow, Bill Bennett, Harry Board, Frank Grigg, John Ireland; front row: William Luscomb (the stationmaster) and Mona Dye.* (PC)

Below: *The first train arriving at the newly-built Bideford station after the extension of the line to Torrington was completed in 1872.*

Right: *Bideford's first train. This scene at the opening of the Bideford Extension Railway in November 1855 was printed in the* Illustrated London News.

Left: *This fine shot of a LSWR engine was taken just in front of the old East-the-Water cemetery chapel.* (PC)

Above: *Bideford railway station during an Edwardian 'rush hour'.* (NDMT

Right: *Frank Grigg in his signal-box at Bideford station – the box still survives and houses a small railway museum.* (PC))

Left and above left: *In 1901 the Town Council was trying to prevent the railway coming along the Quay, and, to out-manoeuvre them, the company directors got their men to lay the line on a Sunday, as shown in these two photographs. The workmen were nearly attacked by the townspeople, the threat only being dissipated by the arrival of a strong force of police.* (PC)

The much-loved Bideford, Westward Ho! and Appledore Railway was opened in April 1901 and closed in 1917. This atmospheric shot clearly shows the steps that allowed passengers to get on and off the trains, there being no platforms as such. (PC)

A typical scene from the 1950s when a steam train drew into Bideford station just below Springfield Terrace – the first sight most visitors would get of Bideford. (PC)

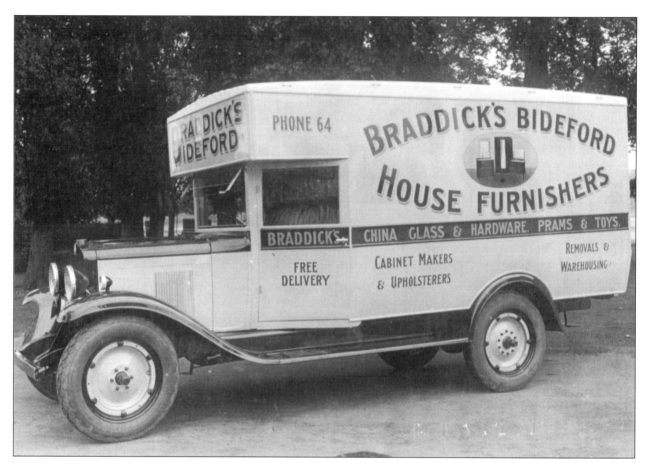

An early goods vehicle on Bideford Quay in the interwar years. (GB)

waiting-room, turntable and locomotive shed, while its predecessor became the goods station. The only major addition after that date was the construction in 1915 of 'Bartlett's Siding', jointly by the local firm of that name and the Ministry of Munitions. This served a munitions factory on the site known at the time of writing as Kynochs.

Bideford had one other railway line – the grandly named Bideford, Westward Ho! and Appledore Railway which, although mooted as early as 1870, only opened in April 1901. Boasting three engines, six coaches (all strictly class-divided) and ten wagons, it was a narrow-gauge railway planned as a loop to join up the three places. Its life was stormy, the Town Council always being at loggerheads with its owners, and passenger traffic was fairly limited.

Indeed its construction was technically illegal as the contractors turned up at 6a.m. on Sunday 7 September 1901 to begin construction on Bideford Quay – without having first obtained the permission they needed. At an emergency council meeting a Councillor Metherall reckoned it 'a most contemptible, unmannerly and mean thing for any company to commence the work on a Sunday in order to obtain a start.' His fellow councillor Mr Friendship went even further and demanded 'that

the ratepayers should present a united front and put their foot on the encroachments of the company forever.' Sensing trouble the police drafted in 30 extra officers and they kept the lid on things – and the company pushed ahead with their line, with the council having to accept the *fait accompli*. In 1917 it was requisitioned by the War Office and disappeared, never to return. One of the few reminders of the line is one of the old engine sheds in Kingsley Road, although at the time of writing this is awaiting conversion from a bus garage into a number of terraced houses.

By the early 1960s rail traffic had declined greatly as car, bus and lorry took over. The death knell was sounded by the Beeching Report of 1963, which recommended the closure of unprofitable branch lines. In October 1965 the last passenger train ran from Barnstaple to Torrington via Bideford, and the use of the line for freight – mainly clay, milk and fertiliser – ceased in September 1982. The last few trains were 'specials' run mainly for railway enthusiasts, and the final train ran in January 1983.

The passenger station is now empty, the old goods yard contains a new estate of local authority houses, and the rails and sleepers have been taken up and replaced by the Tarka Trail, a foot and cycle path.

A spectacular accident in Meddon Street, c.1910. Two uniformed postal messenger boys are among the crowd viewing the stricken steamroller. (AB)

Wickham's staff pose with their delivery vans outside their New Road premises in 1959. Left to right: Frankie Stevens, R. Mitchell, W. Hanwright, Reggie Denford, Basil Pidgeon and F. Branch. (BP)

This amazing photograph from 1917 shows one of the Bideford, Westward Ho! and Appledore Railway engines on its way to the Western Front during the First World War outside the Town Hall prior to crossing the bridge. (HC)

A very unusual sight as a Sunderland Flying Boat lands on the River Torridge with the railway goods yard as a backdrop, some time during the spring of 1939 – the nearest Bideford ever got to having its own airport. (HC)

Chapter 7

Earning a Living

Until the transport 'revolution' of the nineteenth century, Bideford supplied almost all its own needs, so the townsfolk needed many different skills. Although the inhabitants were listed as land-workers in the Domesday Book, many at that time must have turned their hands to other tasks, such as building and clothmaking. As the community grew, specialisation developed; by 1332 there were residents with occupational names like le Hopere (Hooper), le Taillour (Tailor), and Crokker, a word often used for a potter in medieval times. If the men named no longer followed these trades, it is likely that their predecessors in Bideford had done so. Basic needs were also supplied by those who built and repaired houses, or worked wood, metal and leather. The growth of seaborne trade stimulated industry, and by 1540 there was a 'praty quik [pretty lively] Streate of Smithes and other Occupiers for Ship craft' at East-the-Water. Over the next three centuries an increasing number of goods were made in the town, from soap and candles to watches and clocks. In the early-eighteenth century, Bideford had its own tobacco-pipe makers, a cutler, several pewterers, and a mathematical-instrument maker, George Dennys, who worked in the town for about 30 years. There was a living to be made from fishing, too, and many large salmon were caught near the bridge.

Although there was pottery making in medieval Bideford, there is no doubt that its greatest days were in the later-seventeenth and early-eighteenth centuries, when the port was generally more impor-tant than Barnstaple. There was considerable export of North Devon pottery to Wales, Ireland and the American colonies, for example. The industry became so important that some master potters enjoyed the same status as merchants, and one, Thomas Beale, was Mayor in 1658. He, like many later generations of potters, lived in what is now North Road. There were also potteries in Mill Street, at East-the-Water and on the Strand, beside what became known as Potters' Pill, where barges could bring clay up on the tide and load finished wares for transfer to ships at Bideford Quay or Appledore Pool. Some pieces were slipped with white clay, and decorated with lines scratched through to reveal the dark clay beneath. A lead glaze turned these sgraffito wares a rich golden yellow in the kiln and they were very attractive, with their geometrical patterns or designs of flowers and birds. However, plainware, like jars, pitchers and bowls, predominated.

Bideford cloam (clay) ovens, made to build into fireplaces, found a good local market and were also shipped abroad. A fire would be lit inside the oven to heat it and then, after the ashes had been raked out, meat or bread would be sealed in. Such ovens finally went out of use in around 1920. At the peak of production in the 1680s, 290,000 'parcels' (notional pieces) of pottery were shipped out of Bideford annually, and large amounts were also sent inland by road. The number of pots in a parcel depended on size – four one-pint 'penny joogs' for example, or one nine-pint one – but however they were counted, millions of pieces of pottery made in the town contributed to its seventeenth- and early-eighteenth-century prosperity.

Although there were hundreds of later Bideford potters, who kept the industry going for three centuries or more, space makes it impossible to name more than a few. The sister of William Coulscot, a potter in the 1740s, married Joseph Phillips in 1733, and they were probably the parents of John Phillips who was working in Bideford in about 1760, making magnificent 'ship' harvest jugs. Thomas Fields, one of whose jugs was recently sold for thousands of pounds, and whose pieces are dated from 1735–c.1760, appears to have had a connection with him. Phillips signed at least one of his big jugs below the following rhyme, but Fields' name appears on the handle, and no one can be sure who made it. Phillips, who was younger, may have been apprenticed to Fields, or he may have at least worked in the same pottery, perhaps as a decorator, although we shall probably never know. The jug is now in a local museum.

North Road, c.1950. Known locally for many years as Potters Lane, it housed some of the workers in the local pottery-making industry. Although several cottages have been demolished the area retains many of its early houses. (PC)

Above, left to right: *This locally-produced decorated jug and plain, well-made jar and lid, from the seventeenth century, were found in New Street in 1987.* (NDRAU); *Dated 1730, this largest of several dishes bearing the same design was discovered on the site of the Swan Tavern in Chestertown, Maryland, where John Buck and other Bideford merchants had trading connections, and probably came from Bideford.* (CH); *'When men do laber Hard and Swet, good Ale is better far than meet', runs the inscription on the other side of this splendid Bideford harvest jug made by John Phillips in 1775.* (RAMM)

When I was in my native place
 I was a Lumpe of Clay
And Digged up out of the Earth
 And brought from thens away
But now a jug I am become
 By Potters Art and Skill
And I your servant am became
 And Carie Ale I will

John Phillips
1760

In 1766, J. Jewell an Instow potter who may have moved to Bideford later, took on a young apprentice, John Hoyle, whose mother was a Fishley (a name well-known in local potting circles), to learn 'potering' (sic). A century later John Phillips Hoyle was one of the best-known Bideford potters. The name Hoyle is not so common and there may well have been a union of two potting families when his father, Thomas Hoyle, married his mother, Mary Ann Phillips, in 1842. John Phillips Hoyle was the eldest child, baptised the same year as his parents' marriage, so was only 18 in 1860 when he made an excellent ship jug. Two years later he made a very similar jug, but bigger, showing the barque *Ocean Queen*, a transatlantic trader. Both jugs are in a local museum.

Important potters at the end of the eighteenth century included Timothy Goodwin and John Tuckett. However, no known examples of their pottery seem to remain. John, son of Daniel and Elizabeth Bird, was born in 1778 and had a son John Tuckett Bird in 1810. His father may therefore have worked for or with John Tuckett. John Bird was descended from a Huguenot family, originally L'Oiseau. Although his work can be recognised, it is firmly in the North Devon tradition and the Bird family, who had plenty of time to become anglicised, seem to have brought no innovations to the pottery industry.

In the late-eighteenth and early-nineteenth centuries Thomas Barsett was working at Potters' Lane (North Road). He was possibly the maker of a harvest jug now treasured in an American collection. The signature of the maker is almost illegible. He wrote in the clay before it was fired, 'Made in Bideford By Thos Ba...' There follows possibly a long s, and due to an earlier crossing out, there was no more space. The word could be an abbreviation of the name Barsett and the jug was made in 1797, for a Mr Parker. It depicts Ceres, flowers and birds, and has a rhyme under the handle. Another Ceres piece is in the Burton Art Gallery and there appear to have been more, but they are not 'officially' recognised as this potter's work.

William Carder was potting at East-the-Water in the early-nineteenth century, and a descendant of the same name was there at the century's end. The earlier one was from a seafaring family and may have been the master of the *Fanny* trading to Wales, or there was another William Carder even then. The mariner took pottery to sell and brought back lead ore which was used to glaze more pottery. Many potters, including Barsett and Bird, owned vessels (or shares in them), either as an investment or to export their wares.

Thomas Anthony, father and son were, perhaps, the most important potters of the early- and mid-nineteenth century. They apparently left no pieces

This decorated Bideford-made bowl, a rare piece, probably dates from the early-nineteenth century. (RAMM)

Above: One of the oldest East-the-Water public houses, the Blacksmith's Arms. It was later rebuilt and has recently undergone further refurbishment to provide a welcome stop for users of the Tarka Trail. (PC)

Left: The East-the-Water pottery, c.1910. The little boy in the photograph is thought to be Herbie Shortridge. The site later housed Beer's grocery shop. (BL)

Below: Green's well-stocked pottery shop stood where Lloyd's Bank stands at the time of writing and would have sold much produce from the local pottery kilns. It closed in 1891.

Above: *A harvest group from Cadd's Down, c.1910. Note the wicker-bound pottery jars, probably containing cider or beer. The farm has since become an industrial estate.* (SO)

Below: *A trolley loaded with raw materials leaving the culm mine shaft or adit. Note the candle on the front – the only source of illumination.* (NDMT)

Below: *This carefully-posed shot is thought to show the bottling room in the bonded store owned by Wickham's. It is difficult to date but could be from c.1880.* (HC)

The paint mine at East-the-Water when it was operating in the 1930s. (NDMT)

which can be identified. The younger Anthony also owned shares in ships, as well as property on the Strand including what was called the Old Pottery, which bore a seventeenth-century date on one of its chimneys. He married well and his son-in-law, Samuel Crocker, succeeded him. Their contemporaries included John Tucker, father and son, and William Geyton in Potters' Lane. John Tucker junr took a pottery at Cleavehouses by the river for a while.

By 1861 Bryant Ching, locally renowned for his ovens, employed six men and five boys at East-the-Water, and Samuel Crocker had the Old Pottery on the Strand and owned at least one clay pit, as well as the clay quay, as it was now called, at Fremington, from where most of the Bideford potters got their clay. At one time he probably had Ching as his partner. He later moved up to the potters' area in North Road, but kept the name 'Old Pottery'. No one else approached Samuel Crocker's social status, which in some ways equalled that of the Beales in the seventeenth century. W.H. Crocker, his son, succeeded him, but died in 1876, and the pottery was sold.

By this time there was a little simple machinery. For example, each pottery had a pug mill and some had a (drain)pipe-making machine. As well as 'pounding troughs', kiln rakes and fire pikes, coarse wares such as ovens and salters appeared prominently among the goods in stock. There must have been a market for them, for Bideford in 1861 still had 18 'earthenware manufacturers' (including all who worked in potteries, not merely master potters). The beginning of the end could be seen, however, for in the 1820s there had been eight potteries in Bideford, and in the 1850s there were only five. At the end of the century, Crocker's was bought and was later run by one Milton, who has been described as 'an unsuccessful potter who made coarse common ware', and who soon gave up. Then only the pottery at Torrington Lane, East-the-Water remained. It was run by James Redcliffe or Redclift who was born in 1833 or '34, and Henry Phillips (of the potting family) who was born in 1835. The latter worked most of his life at East-the-Water and perhaps made the last Bideford harvest jugs. Redcliffe's career was also at East-the-Water. Latterly, his staff included James

Davis, to whom he sold the pottery on his retirement in 1911. The sale of the lease included Prince, the pottery horse that worked the pug mill, at £1 per leg, or £4 altogether! Some plain ware by Davis is in the Burton Art Gallery and Museum. It is perhaps typical of most Bideford pottery of the late-nineteenth and early-twentieth centuries – plain, serviceable and lacking artistic merit. The industry was now failing due to competition from lighter and more up-to-date materials – enamel and galvanised iron, for instance, for many utensils. The First World War, with only unskilled Belgian refugees for the work-force, dealt it the death blow, and the last traditional pottery in Bideford closed in 1916.

The Bideford pottery industry grew large in the seventeenth century and flourished with the tobacco trade into the eighteenth, until war drove the trade away from Bideford. At the same time the Bideford merchants, who had often shipped pottery with more important goods to Ireland and America, died out, and Bideford lost its pre-eminence as a port.

As society developed, however, demand arose for the services of lawyers, surgeons and surveyors such as Nathaniel Gascoyne, who planned Bridgeland Street. Many men were employed in building the street, including Samuel Curtice, a mason, and William Lynex or Lynch, a brickmaker, both of whom later lived there, as did Gascoyne himself. Other residents were merchants and 'gentlemen' like Peter Glubb, an attorney, who also owned land locally. He dabbled in shipowning and foreign trade and was four times Mayor of Bideford between 1719 and 1747. Extracts from a domestic account book he kept for many years illustrate the range of services and locally-made goods available then:

	£	s	d
Pd Tom Cane for dressing a skin			3
Pd John Cole for Shoes for Blanch			
(his daughter)		7	6
Gave Mr Christopher Bedford for curing			
my child		10	6
Pd for engraven my Seal		7	0
Pd Sampson Hole for a wig		2 2	0
Pd Mr Beale a quarter's shaving		1 1	0
Pd Thomas Pyke for my gown		7 3	6
Pd George Stanbury for a horse		7 0	0
Pd Tom Harris for looking after my horse		10	0
Pd Richard Cole ye sadler		14	6
Pd Robert Saunders for curing my gray			
mare and my horse's bad leg		1 4	6
Pd Mr Finney for a spoon		12	0

James Finney was one of several goldsmiths then working in Bideford. Some, like Henri and Francois Servante, were among the Huguenots who came to Bideford when driven from France by Louis XIV's religious persecution. They included doctors, craftsmen who 'carried on the silk and cotton manufactures', and

Below: *Wickham's wine stores on the corner of High Street and Grenville Street dates from the 1830s. It was still operating until nearly the end of the twentieth century.*

Above: *Dawe's large grocery store at the corner of High Street and Mill Street. In 1905 it was bought by the Wiltshire & Dorset Bank, becoming Lloyd's during the First World War. In 1927 it passed to Barclays, which it still is at the time of writing.*

The Commercial Bank, one of the earliest in Bideford, issued its own £5, £2 and £1 notes. (PC)

Left: *The plate-glass windows that revolutionised shopping are well illustrated in this view looking up High Street from c.1900. The curious fittings on the first shop are designed to reflect light back onto the window displays. No parking problems in those days!* (PC)

Above left: *The Heavitree Arms in Mill Street is still a busy public house in the early-twenty-first century. It is seen here c.1900.* (BL)

Above: *At the time of writing this building houses the offices of Torridge District Council, but this shot, dating from c.1910, shows when it was known as Westcombe Tannery works. The industry, which was rather noisome, has long disappeared from the town.* (AB)

Above: *Women workers at their machines inside the Westcombe Collar Factory, c.1900. Bundles of collars lie beside the men in the 'office'.* (NDMT)

Right: *An Edwardian butcher's shop in High Street next to where the TSB was located until 2004. Note the delivery boy and his bicycle to the right.* (DT)

Chope's, the largest shop in the High Street, advertises a 'Rebuilding Sale' between the wars. The old frontage was completely altered in 1987. (PC)

A butcher's shop at East-the-Water, along with the owner's delivery cart. The building has since been demolished to form part of the Royal Hotel's car park. It is surmounted by an 'eagle' produced in Bideford. (PC)

merchants and mariners who 'considerably enlarged the circle of Bideford's commerce'.

Some of Bideford's older industries, such as pottery, shipbuilding and limeburning, continued into the nineteenth century. Five limekilns are shown on an 1842 map of the town and one of these (in a builder's yard in New Road) survives, albeit covered by later building. The culm pits were re-opened and the soft, 'rotted' product made into a paint called Bideford Black. An 1811 sales catalogue for the Union Mine at the junction of High Street and Gunstone noted:

It has lately been introduced into His Majesty's Navy as a Paint with much Success; it is also applicable to paying Ship's Bottoms, and all the purposes of a dry black Colour; and has received the countenance and support, not only of the first Artists, but of the most respectable Manufacturers in all parts of the Kingdom.

Other mine adits, one of which was over 1,000 feet long by the 1830s, were behind what is now the Grenville Nursing Home in Meddon Street, and at Pillhead and Chapel Park, East-the-Water, whence the culm was taken down to a special wharf by an overhead tramway. In the mid-nineteenth century, 27 Bideford men were recorded as working in the paint business. The work was still dangerous and the graves of men who died in mine accidents can be seen in Old Town Cemetery. The last working mine, employing three men in what is at the time of writing the Bideford Scrap Metals yard, closed in 1969.

After 1812 the occupations of fathers whose children were baptised had to be recorded in parish registers. Between 1813 and 1822, the 1,000 or so Bideford entries show the majority of these men in manufacturing. A total of 57 entries refer to shipwrights, 28 to potters, 30 to blacksmiths, 70 to shoemakers and 29 to other leather workers. Also included in the entries

are 163 'labourers', 88 mariners and 60 masons, seven teachers, six tax-collectors, three watchmakers and one comedian. However, the registers do record some men, and therefore their occupations, more than once, as they had more than one child baptised during the period. It should also be remembered that these 'statistics' exclude men without young children, nonconformists and women.

Women had contributed to Bideford's economy through the ages, although in early times only a few rich widows enjoyed independence. In the early-fifteenth century, Alice Cadd owned land (at Caddsdown, presumably named after the family), and often acted as a witness to legal transactions, along with leading townsmen. Sybil Andrew, in Elizabethan times, was one of a number of merchants' widows who conducted their late husbands' affairs. In 1676, 15 widows were among the town's alehouse keepers, and women who had worked with husbands or fathers sometimes took over businesses, such as Mary Prance, a pipemaker in 1703, and Patience Sincombe, a potter 30 years later. Martha Burnard carried on as a shipowner after her husband's death in 1824, but went bankrupt ten years later. The majority of women working outside their own homes were in service. Women who worked in Peter Glubb's household got their board and £2 or £3 a year, half the men's rate. He paid a nanny 12s. for a short period of residence, and the midwife £1.6s. for a lying-in. She was called 'nurse' and had to have some practical skills at least. For a time a licence from the church was also needed, and a letter of recommendation survives from 1699:

*This is to certify that Jackett Blackmore of Bideford is well scilled in the Office of a Midwife And that she is well aproved of them that make use of her
Signed Humphrey Ackland. Churchwarden.*

Left: *Many photographs have captions noting that the buildings shown have now been demolished. Here we see demolition in progress. The Quayside site was being cleared in 1936 prior to the new HQ of the Bideford Building Society being constructed. In 2004 the building houses the offices of Business Link.* (HC)

Right: *Bideford's role as a market centre was carried on in the twentieth century by mobile food merchants such as George Beer, a grocer in Honestone Street. Here he is seen with his delivery van in the 1930s.* (RD)

Right: *This fine building is still recognisable in 2005 as part of Braddick's furniture shop in Mill Street.* (GB)

Below: *For many years the Pridham family was involved in the coaching trade and this shop in Grenville Street, selling saddles and other leather goods, grew from that business.* (NDMT)

Above: *Mill Street at its junction with Bridgeland Street, c.1910. The wonderfully florid wall advertisements show a keen entrepreneurial sense, whilst the shop in the middle of the photograph is selling postcards – some of which probably feature in this book.* (BL)

Below right: *Mill Street at its junction with Bridgeland Street, c.1900. Mr Barrett, a printer, ran the shop on the left and in his window can be seen various photographs and specimens of his work.* (BL)

Below: *Woodyatt's grocery shop was situated in this building (which still survives at the time of writing) at the top of High Street.* (AW)

Right: *This shop at the junction of High Street and the Quay is not easily recognisable in 2004, now that its frontage has changed so dramatically. The 'greenhouse' on the roof was a photographer's studio.* (PC)

Below: *The interior of Wickham's wine merchants at the corner of High and Grenville Streets in 1959. Left to right: Basil Pidgeon, R. Hallam, Mrs M. Westlake, Stanley Fogaty and Frank Snow.* (BP)

E. GERRISH, M.P.S.
(Late Tovey & Underwood),
Dispensing and Photographic Chemist
(By Examinations),
9, Quay (Corner of High Street.), **BIDEFORD.**

Prescriptions Accurately Dispensed,
Personal Attention.
Aerated Waters in Syphons.   Mineral Waters in Bottles
Turkey, Honeycomb and India Rubber Sponges
Hair Brushes and Toilet Articles of every description.
Elastic Stockings, Anklets, Kneecaps, always in Stock.
Perfumes, finest qualit es imported direct.

DARK=ROOM, DEVELOPING AND PRINTING,
PHOTOGRAPHIC REQUISITES.

8972   36

Tattersill's Stores

HIGH-CLASS
Teas, Groceries & Provisions.

Price List on application.

Daily Deliveries by our own Vans to
Northam, Westward Ho! and Neighbourhood.
13 & 14, Market Place,
8, High Street,
1, Grenville Street,
20, Mill Street,
Telephone No. 28   **BIDEFORD.**
8

Left: *A lovely interior view of one of the town's grocery shops. E. Tattersill was a very successful Mayor in the Edwardian period who died relatively young.* (PC)

Below: *This unusual interior view shows the Rola Works in April 1956. The factory was moved here during the Second World War to produce top-secret components for the RAF and occupied the site where Safeways stands at the time of writing.* (NDJ)

63

Looking up Bridge Street in 1897. On the left is Wolland's hairdressing shop and to the right is William's cycle shop. (RC)

Over the centuries, many poorer women added to the family income by spinning yarn at home. As late as 1800 some Bideford women and children were thus employed by William Shepherd, a Plymouth wool manufacturer but, even with wages as low as 3s.4d. a week, handmade products could not compete with machine-made goods from the north of England, and this employment died away after the Napoleonic Wars (post 1815). In Bideford itself 'small manufactories of flannel and serges' struggled on into the 1830s, before what had for centuries been one of the town's leading trades disappeared. Bideford had no coal and iron, so the local merchant who in 1849 said, 'West country people must borrow some of the energy and boldness of their northern neighbours if they would ever become as prosperous as they might be', had missed a basic point.

In times of hardship the poor had to ask the parish for 'relief' and many records of this help still exist. In 1835–36 the town built a new workhouse in Meddon Street to provide accommodation for 200 paupers. It was run by the Board of Guardians who met regularly to dispense punishment to troublesome inmates and to scrutinize carefully the accounts to see that the residents were not being pampered. It lasted until 1948 when the NHS was set up and did away with the old and much-hated workhouse system.

The 1851 census provides a complete picture of the occupational structure of the town, before the railway brought the needed 'stimulant to improvement'. Manufacturing, with nearly 900 people involved, was still dominant in Bideford, but individual trades were declining. Only three brewers worked in the town and, although there were 70 shipwrights, 19 ropemakers, one anchorsmith, and a number of general labourers, painters and carvers, shipbuilding was not so important as formerly. Women, however, had become an important part of the workforce, with 153 listed as dressmakers and 47

as milliners. A total of 75 more were employed in glovemaking which, using cheap manual labour, was one of the few local growth industries. Women also formed the majority of the 555 servants, the men in this category being gamekeepers and gardeners. Richer families often had cook, housemaid, childsmaid and nurse, and even small artisans could afford a 'skivvy'. There were 190 people engaged in agriculture, many on the outlying farms in the parish, but a sizeable number lived in the town itself, within walking distance of fields not yet built over, for this was before the days when bricks could be cheaply transported from elsewhere. In 1851 Bideford was still predominantly a town of stone and cob houses but, as well as many masons and carpenters, there were three local brickmakers and one bricklayer. Meanwhile, in this pre-railway age, the biggest single employer was a coaching firm, with 60 men.

Civil service and local government were still in embryonic form, and in 1851 the town managed to function with only 19 'public officials'. Although there were fewer services then, Bideford was evidently becoming something of a retirement centre, with 162 mainly elderly people listed in the census as 'property owners and of independent means'. The decline of this small, self-contained community into 'decayed gentility' with no modern industry was averted by two arrivals – Charles Kingsley in 1854, and the railway a year later. Inspired by the former and transported by the latter, a great flow of tourists came to see the 'little white town' described in *Westward Ho!* Remarkable development then took place and a locally printed guidebook from 1856 talks of the:

Another splendidly decorated shop appears in this photograph of F. Perkins' greengrocery which was on the Quay where the Portland Building Society now stands.

... speculators in house building and proprietors, who, of late years, have beautified the town of Bideford with elegant erections for families of distinction, the splendid modern shop windows, and the many tasteful mansions and villas in its vicinity.

The same writer also boasted of the 'cleanliness, convenience and comfort' of the town. In 1894 a later guidebook added, 'No town in the West of England has grown so rapidly, and few have been so radically improved.'

The list of Bideford's improvements over the next 30 or 40 years is breathtaking – the Parish Church, apart from the tower, rebuilt in 1862–64/65; the Long Bridge widened from 15 feet to 24 feet at a cost of £6,000 in 1865; the Music Hall built in Bridgeland Street in 1869; the town completely resewered in 1871, and the railway extended to Torrington the next year. Several more schools were opened, a library was established in 1875, the imposing Bridge Buildings were erected in 1882, the Pannier Market in 1883–84, and the first purpose-built hospital in 1887. In 1889, St Peter's Church at East-the-Water was opened, and the Quay was widened. All this, together with private rebuilding schemes, provided employment for many townspeople.

One of the most important nineteenth-century developments was the introduction of collar making. The first of three large factories was opened at Westcombe in 1871, and many from Bideford and the surrounding villages were soon working in this industry. It was noted that 'the wages earned by all these people, and spent by them amongst the traders of the town, are no inconsiderable item in the making of Bideford.' For a variety of reasons the population of the town had risen from 2,987 in 1801 to 7,875 in 1891, so shops also grew in number, size and range of goods offered. By the mid-nineteenth century, the first plate-glass windows had been installed, and soon a local writer could say, 'it is no flattery to the tradesmen to say that they have the best stocks in any class of goods this side of Exeter, at any rate.' The Pannier Market established a reputation for fresh food and colourful displays, and the Market Place was opened up as a shopping area. Local farmers could now send dairy produce away by rail before it spoilt.

As tourism expanded so did the number of hotels. Some writers described Bideford's as 'of the highest order and respectability', but one famous visitor disagreed. 'My dearest Georgy,' wrote Charles Dickens in a letter headed:

Bideford, North Devon,
Thursday night, first November 1860
I write (with the most impracticable iron pen on earth) to report our safe arrival here, in a beastly hotel. We had stinking fish for dinner, and have been able to drink nothing, though we have ordered wine, beer and brandy-and-water. There is nothing in the house but

two tarts and a pair of snuffers. The landlady is playing cribbage with the landlord in the next room (behind a thin partition), and they seem quite comfortable...

The New Inn (one of the oldest in Bideford and in 2004 sadly due for redevelopment as flats) was for many years the centre of a thriving coaching service. At one time it housed its own brewery using an underground stream flowing down Honestone Street and Bridge Street. In the nineteenth century, when Bidefordians spoke of the 'Pack of Cards' they meant not one inn, but the total number of pubs, supposed to be 52, but since then the proportion of hostelries to population has declined. Of four nineteenth-century inns on the Quay, only the King's Arms remains. The Newfoundland Hotel, made famous by Kingsley as the Ship Tavern, is now a fish-and-chip shop.

The 1901 census reveals a very different settlement from that of 50 years before. Manufacturing still dominated the town but this was down to the one industry of collar making which employed 569 (mainly women) – a total swelled by large numbers of workers who travelled in every day from Northam and Appledore. Shipbuilding had all but disappeared, only eight potters are listed as still working in the town and agricultural workers had declined to 89.

The largest 'new' group, apart from the collar workers, were the railwaymen. Some 64 are listed in the census and their presence highlights the revolution in transport that occurred in Queen Victoria's reign. The growth in social services saw the Dispensary or hospital in Meddon Street having five live-in staff looking after 19 patients, whilst the workhouse just up the road housed 56 adult paupers, 24 children and nine 'casuals' or tramps. Various other new occupations are listed including cycle fitters and dealers, bottlers of soda water, photographers, antique dealers, an 'Electrical Engine Driver', an artificial-teeth maker, and even Venitia Donati, a 22-year-old telephone operator living in High Street.

Kingsley Hospital at East-the-Water was built as an isolation unit and later became a centre for autistic children. (PC)

As might be expected the number of servants had shrunk – down to 431 or less than five per cent of the total, when half a century before they had made up nearly ten per cent of the population. Such staff were only to be found now in the outlying farms or the large new houses in Abbotsham Road. The grandest house was that of Louisa Stucley, the 60-year-old widow of an MP who had nine domestic staff to serve her needs at Moreton House. For the most part, however, Bideford was rapidly assuming the trappings of a modern twentieth-century town.

In fact these changes in industry and transport benefited Bideford in many ways, but killed industries which could neither mechanise nor compete with mass-produced goods from elsewhere. Mention has already been made of the closure of the last traditional Bideford pottery in 1916, but since then Bideford-built ships and even the railway itself have become things of the past, with the toy factory at Handy Cross disappearing along with 'Supreme Magic' in the High Street. Following the decline of 'traditional' trades, Bideford people in the twentieth century have pursued occupations ranging from archaeology to zookeeping, and today there are computer shops as well as 'New Age' outlets, along with some handsome new developments such as 'Crabby Dicks' in Cooper Street. In addition there is the ultra-modern Safeway store as well as a massive out-of-town shopping development at Atlantic Village and Clovelly Road. Change is certainly a constant in Bideford.

Above: 'Manchester House' stood at the corner of North Road and Chingswell Street and sold a huge range of ready-made clothing. It was later rebuilt, becoming Yeo's, and at the time of writing houses a pet shop.

Above: A close-up of Woodyatt's window in around 1930, highlighting how dependent our ancestors were on candles for illumination. Note the chewing-gum machine to the left. (PU)

Above: When Wickham's wine shop was built at the corner of High and Grenville Street, in around 1830, a seam of culm was discovered and worked. The exhausted adit was then converted to a series of basements and Wickham's later used one for bottling beer – as shown in this photograph from 1959. Left to right: H. Pidgeon, H. Holman, J. Hancock, K. Tanton and A. Brock. (BP)

Right: Grimes & Co. had their jeweller's shop in High Street and it is lucky for Bideford that their ornate shopfront still survives in the early-twenty-first century – with the name Grimes worked in mosaic in the doorway.

One of the oldest drapery businesses in the town – Vellacott, Trapnell & Merefield of High Street. At the time of writing the site is occupied by an accountancy business. (BL)

Right: *An advertisement from c.1900 for W. Foot, a visiting dentist.* (PC)

Below: *This evocative snap dated 1914 shows the corner of Willet Street and Mill Street with two shop men in their long aprons. To the right is a newsagent's. In 2004 Braddick's video shop and the Blue Dolphin fish-and-chip restaurant occupied the sites.*

Mr. W. Foot,

Surgeon Dentist,

MARKET PLACE, BIDEFORD,

Begs to inform the Clergy, Gentry and Inhabitants of Bideford and Neighbourhood that he has commenced Practice over the new premises of Messrs. Heywood & Sons, Musical Instrument Salesmen, Market Place, Bideford, where attendance daily will be given from 9 a.m. to 8 p.m.

Mr. W. Foot having had 15 years experience with some of the West End, London, Dentists; and for some time Manager and Operator for Mr. Passmore, of Exeter, feels confident he will give every satisfaction to patients who place themselves in his hands for professional services.

He also wishes to inform the Inhabitants that the Artificial Teeth supplied by him are precisely the same as supplied by other dentists at a much higher price; and that every case undertaken by him is guaranteed a perfect fit.

LIST OF FEES.

	£.	s.	d.		£.	s.	d.
A single tooth on Vulcanite plate		3	6	A Complete set upper & lower on Best			
A single tooth on Best Vulcanite plate		5	0	Vulcanite Plate	5	5	0
A single tooth on Platinum Plate		7	6	Teeth filled from		2	6
A single tooth on Gold Plate		12	6	Teeth filled with White Enamel Filling		5	0
A complete set upper & lower on Vulcanite				Teeth extracted		1	0
Plate		3	3	0	Teeth extracted by gas, including Doctor's Fee	15	0

No charge will be made for Extractions when Artificial Teeth are required.
ALL CONSULTATIONS FREE.

Above left: *F. Karslake's millinery and drapery shop was situated at 62a Mill Street. Here advertising an 'Early Spring Sale', it brought the latest fashions to its provincial customers.*

Above right: *An unusual sight in a town – a local hunt crosses the bridge, c.1920. They were probably from the country around Bideford, for few townspeople would have had the money or leisure for hunting.* (NDMT)

Right: *People may think the coffee shop is a new thing, but this advertisement from c.1890 shows that Bideford could boast at least one such establishment during the reign of Victoria.* (PC)

Below: *This fine shot is said to show one of the 'Hungarian Bands' that performed in Bideford during the summer to please the tourists.* (PC)

KINGDON'S
TEA & COFFEE WAREHOUSE,
(The Golden Canister),
2, BUTT-GARDEN STREET,
BIDEFORD.

WILLIAM KINGDON, in thanking the Clergy, Gentry, and Inhabitants generally of Bideford and neighbourhood, for the extensive patronage bestowed by them on his late Father (Mr. Abraham Kingdon), during the past 19 years, begs to solicit a continuance of the same, and to say that it will be his study to continue to supply Teas and Coffees of exceptional value, so as to maintain the high reputation gained by his late Father.

The Business will in future be carried on under the name of

A. KINGDON & SON.

Try our CELEBRATED TEAS.
At 1/8, 2/-, 2/6 and 3/- per lb.

Also, our Pure Fresh ROASTED COFFEES (whole or ground),
At 1/4 and 1/8 per lb.

☞ NOTE THE ADDRESS—
2, BUTT-GARDEN STREET, BIDEFORD.

W. C. CHAPP, Machine Printer, 'Gazette' Office, Bideford.

Chapter 8

Domestic Diversions

Few references are found to everyday life in Bideford before the seventeenth century, and subsequently the lives of the rich are better documented than those of the poor. Most leisure pursuits date from modern times, due to shorter working hours and labour-saving devices.

Bideford's weekly market sold 'flesh and fruit of all sorts', dairy produce was plentiful, and in 1685 a Huguenot refugee noted that a loaf as wide as a plate cost only $^1/_2$d. Much fish was eaten and the Bridge Trustees justified holding fish dinners on the grounds that the consumption of dried cod helped the Newfoundland fisheries. Bideford ships brought in such luxuries as dried and fresh citrus fruits, white sugar, spices, marmalade, chocolate and liquorice for the rich, who had dishes of pewter, fine china, or even silver, and drank wine from delicate Venetian glasses. Tea later became fashionable, but in 1724 one pound of it cost as much as two gallons of brandy. Ordinary folk had a plainer diet, drank beer or cider, and used wooden trenchers and earthenware bowls. In 1673 Bideford had 35 pauper households, and a century later 60 people were in the workhouse, which spent £215 a year on their food. They were allowed 1lb of bread a day, 3lbs of 'flesh' a week, and some bacon, dried peas and milk. Their diet was probably supplemented with vegetables and fruit from the workhouse garden and they brewed their own beer.

Modern houses are full of electrical goods and comfortable furnishings, and Victorians often crammed their houses with furniture and ornaments, but their ancestors possessed fewer household goods. Although she owned linen and other items of some value, the only furniture in the house of Sir Richard Grenville's widow, Lady Mary, who died in Bideford in 1623, consisted of a 'Cheste and Truncke' valued at £3, a 'Boarde [table] and Bedsteads' (£2) and 'Formes and stooles' (£2). Richard Sherman, a merchant who made his will in 1646, had more things – 'table boards', a sideboard, a cupboard, feather beds, spruce and cypress chests, and two scriptories (for writing). He also listed his 'best greene carpett', 'best looking glass', and an 'Indyan quilt'.

In the seventeenth century clothing was kept until it wore out. Richard Sherman stored his first wife's clothes after her death and finally willed them to relatives. They included a beaver hat, a 'grogram' cloak, a riding suit, a best gown, her best petticoats

Once Sir Bevil Grenville's town house, the Three Tuns was for many years one of four public houses on the Quay. Extensively rebuilt, it houses a skateboard and cycling shop at the time of writing.

Typical of the many small public houses found in Bideford was the Old Ring of Bells in Honestone Street. Completely rebuilt it has continued as a public house under various names but in 2004 is empty. (PC)

Above and left: *Bideford Regatta in 1951. Huge crowds watch the races and the river is crowded with craft dressed in flags in honour of the occasion.* (NDJ)

Below: *Bideford's brass bands have long been famous and in April 1951 the local newspaper was proud to feature this Champion Silver Band.* (NDJ)

Left: *The Music Hall in Bridgeland Street became the Palace Cinema. In the early-nineteenth century the Grammar School master lived and taught here; in the seventeenth century merchant John Smith's house was here.* (PC)

Above: *Turner's tea and coffee shop in Buttgarden Street, c.1900, which was later replaced by the Edelweiss Hotel. The roof of the New Inn is in the background, as is the quirky triangular house at the top of Tower Street.* (BL)

Right: *The coronation of Queen Elizabeth saw fierce competition to produce the best decorations. This scene from June 1953 shows a resplendent Union Street (off Allhalland Street).* (NDJ)

Below: *Coronations have always seen a wonderful array of celebratory events in Bideford – fitting perhaps for a town whose motto is 'Pro Rege Ac Fide Audax', which translates as 'Bold for King and Faith'.* (PC)

THURSDAY, JUNE 26, 1902

10.15 a.m.

PUBLIC MEETING at the Town Hall. Presentation by the Mayor to the Corporation, on behalf of the donors, of ten new Links to the Mayor's Chain.

The following Gentlemen have each contributed a Link:

Mr. A. L. Restarick, in Memory of the late Mr. Alderman Restarick.
Mr. Alderman Dymond, J.P.
Mr. Alderman Ascott, J.P.
Mr. Alderman Narraway, J.P., C.C.
Friends of the late Mr. Alderman Braund.
Mr. Councillor Goaman, J.P.
Mr. H. M. Bazeley, Clerk of the Peace.
Mr. W. R. Seldon, Town Clerk.
Mr. M. R. Gooding, Medical Officer of Health
Mr. F. A. Searle, Borough Treasurer.

PRESENTATION by the Mayor of a Medallion Portrait of King Edward VII., as a centrepiece to the new links in commemoration of the Coronation of His Majesty.

VOTE OF THANKS—
Proposed by Mr. Alderman Cock.
Seconded by Mr. Councillor Stanley Heard.

☞ A Congratulatory TELEGRAM will be sent to the King by the Mayor on behalf of the Inhabitants of the Borough.

10.45 a.m.

PROCESSION to the Park of the Mayor and Corporation, Magistrates, Borough Officials; Members of Friendly and kindred Societies; the E & H Companies, with Band, of the 4th V.B.D.R., in Command of Captain Martin and Officers; the Hungarian Military Season Band, under Herr A. Groop; by kind permission of Lord Ebrington, Col. Commanding, Members of the D Squadron R. N. D. Hussars; and the Church Lads' Brigade.

THURSDAY, JUNE 26, CONTINUED.

11 a.m.

Presentation by the Mayor of Flag Staff and Flags at the Park.

Hoisting of Union Jack by Miss Violet Tattersill.

National Anthem by the Band, and a Feu-de-Joie by the Volunteers.

VOTE OF THANKS—
Proposed by Mr. Ald. Narraway, J.P., C.C.
Seconded by Mr. Councillor Pollard.

11.15 a.m.

Procession will re-form and proceed to the Parish Church.

11.30 a.m.

COMMEMORATION SERVICE at the Parish Church, conducted by the Rector, the Rev. T. Newton Leeke.

Broad Quay after Divine Service. Presentation by the Mayor of Bars to the Volunteers that have served in South Africa, viz.:—

Lance-Corpl. S. Fulford. Privates E. J. Lee, W. W. Turner, J. Tucker, J. Shortridge, C. Shaxon.

1.30 p.m.

A FREE DINNER will be provided in the Market for all holders of Tickets.

Hungarian Military Season Band in attendance.

The Loyal Toasts will be submitted by the Mayor.

Travelling fairs were a common sight on the Quay or the Pill. This boxing booth is roughly where the bowling club is in Chingswell Street in 2005. (NDMT)

Above: *A proud winning team from 1923. Both the Amateur Athletics Club and the Amateur Rowing Club are still very active at the time of writing.* (PC)

Right: *Bideford has long been famous for its rowing teams and here we see a crew loading their boats in 1952.* (NDJ)

Below: *Some billboards beside the Bideford Amateur Athletic Club advertise the Palace Cinema and various foods in the 1930s.* (PC)

Below: *The 1926 West of England Amateur Rowing Association Junior Championship was won by the Bideford Amateur Rowing Club, and this photograph was commissioned by the Mayor to record the victory. Left to right, back row: C. Morris, F. Montague, F. Gayette, S. Morris (cox), J. Schillers, R. Hocking (stroke), J. Mitchell; front row: E. Day (secretary), H. Stucley (president), J. Metherell (Mayor), S. Lake (vice-captain).* (BARC)

with green velvet laces, her second-best petticoat, a 'blanched silk apron lined with ley and bound about' and another silk apron, as well as one of black 'stuff'. The merchant himself possessed three suits; his best suit, which he did not describe further, one of 'melley' (medley) cloth, which may have been colourful, and one of black stuff, which was probably for everyday use. He also had a pair of silk stockings and garters, a silk scarf, three cloaks, a greatcoat and a long blue cape. Rings never went out of fashion, and he listed his signet ring and seven more rings, as well as 11 pieces of plate and six silver spoons. Like the merchant's widow, Sybil Andrew, who died over 60 years before him, Richard Sherman set great store by cooking utensils, leaving a kettle and three brass crocks or pans. These were still quite valuable. He also left a tar kettle, but this was hardly kitchenware – perhaps he used it to tar a vessel. There are signs that he had been a mariner, for many merchants rose that way, and he left his 'asterlaby instrument' to John Boole, another Bideford mariner turned merchant. He also left a fowling piece, which was kept at Northam, so the place was probably marshy then and perhaps had many wildfowl. His interest in the Newfoundland trade has already been mentioned, and he left his cellar (or storehouse) on the Quay at Bideford to the Mayor and Corporation, in trust for the poor. He seems to have had no children (at least no surviving ones), and he left all his lands and buildings in Bideford to a rich Bristol merchant's son, perhaps his nephew or great-nephew, for he was also called Sherman. There are signs that these relations began as North Devon merchants who did well enough to move to a big city, which was quite common then, even though Richard Sherman ended his days in Bideford.

A number of rich people's houses survive from the seventeenth century onwards, some of them retaining their original plaster ceilings, carved wooden staircases and overmantels, but in 1730 Peter Glubb employed a stonemason to make 'ye Chimley peice in ye Parlour' of his Bridgeland Street house. In this later century rich people were even more fashion conscious, and he bought earrings and a muff for his daughter, new wigs for himself, and many different types of cloth, including 17 yards of green mantua silk, which cost him £4.17s.9d. As for furniture, increasing wealth and outside contacts brought new fashions in the eighteenth century, but provincial craftsmen made copies to order, so Peter Glubb had his 'horse foot table and Iland table' made in Bideford in 1730 at a cost of £2.3s. The nineteenth century brought mass-produced cheap cloth and a brisk trade for drapers, especially when voluminous skirts came into fashion. Many milliners and 'straw hat makers' were needed in those days.

Some old cottages remain, much altered, but many have been replaced by terraces of durable yellow brick, one of the features of local nineteenth-century development. With the increase in population, housing estates of a number of periods and styles have been built around the original settlements, on both sides of the river.

It is recorded that in 1635 there were 24 alehouses in Bideford, so there was at least one well-supported leisure activity in the town. No doubt more drinking took place on special occasions, such as the celebration of a successful English attack on the Dutch coast in 1666, when:

... the mayor and his brethren appeared at divine service in their scarlet robes, and Mr Gifford, a worthy divine performed duty, after which 70 guns were fired, drums beat and bells rang till 11 at night.

A quieter recreation, smoking, had become popular by this time, and there was no shortage of tobacco in the port of Bideford. Clay pipes were made locally and also imported from Holland, but in the eighteenth century, gentlemen chose to take their tobacco another way, Peter Glubb paying 6s.6d. for 'snuff and a canister' in 1724.

In 1608 the Bridge Trust was accused of spending its funds on 'entertaining of strangers and in banquetting and often feasting between themselves, and also for the seeing of stage plays acted within the Town of Bydeford.' Thereafter, the puritan element may, as in neighbouring towns, have paid touring players to go away! There is no more evidence of public entertainments until 1775, when the Bridge Trust converted the Fox and Goose, an old inn on the site of what is today Grenville House on the Quay, to the 'Mayor's House'. Also known as the Assembly Rooms or Mansion House, this was practically the only building available in the town for balls, concerts, lectures and such entertainments as a 'casino' with a cabaret entitled *The Evening Duffer*, which was received with 'loud bursts of applause' in 1794.

Later in 1794, James Biggs of Barnstaple, an actor-manager, presented *Richard III* and *The Irishman in London*, in a new theatre in Bideford. This may also have been the scene of the benefit performance in 1798 by Mr Harper's Company of Comedians, 'for the families of the brave seamen who fell in the late glorious victory' (the Battle of the Nile). It was perhaps 'the late theatre on the Quay' mentioned in 1808. In 1822 a newspaper reported that:

Mr Lee, Manager of the Taunton and Bridgwater Theatres has, we hear, opened an elegant little Theatre with a select but respectable Dramatic Corps at Bideford.

This theatre could have been a temporary structure, for two years later it was reported that Lee's Company of Comedians was to play in Bideford's Old Corn

Left: *The Swan Inn was a well-known public house in Mill Street on the site of what is Vinnie's Café in 2004. The resplendent figure in this photograph, from c.1890, is thought to be the town crier.* (PC)

Below: *The old warehouse at the end of Rope Walk that became the Bideford Amateur Rowing Club HQ in 1936 and on its opening day.* (BARC)

Below: *Bideford Regatta remains one of the high spots of the town's sporting calendar – but horseracing on the river sands at low tide no longer occurs as it did in this photograph from August 1908. The winning horse was Pretty Polly, owned by Mr Hernaman and ridden by Mr Tucker.* (SO)

Market for a month. In 1825, the newly-started *North Devon Journal* reported from Bideford that:

... a Theatre is to be built, so we hear, near the New Buildings to contain 5 or 600 people. Subscriptions have been entered into, and nearly the whole estimated expense of the building is already raised.

Subsequent *Journal* copies are missing, so it is not certain whether this building was erected, although there were Subscription Rooms on the Quay.

Other entertainments in Bideford included a 'Panorama of the Battles of Navarino and Algiers' in 1828, with admission prices ranging from $2^1/_2$d. to $7^1/_2$d. Song recitals were popular – in 1829 the Raines family of the Tyrol gave a series of concerts, and in 1832 the Oxfordshire Minstrels performed before 'the principal part of the town and neighbouring gentry.' Two child prodigies put on 'The diorama of Shakespeare's jubilee' in the same year, and in 1833 a book of actors' reminiscences attracted 18 Bideford subscribers. In 1831 and 1835 Wombwell's Menagerie came to Bideford, and travelling circuses visited the town throughout the nineteenth century, often in Fair Week.

Amateur performances became popular in the nineteenth century. In 1825, John Handford, a local chemist:

... raised an Amateur Company of Comedians, who performed several philanthropic pieces at the Bush Tavern [in High Street]... *to the great and novel amusement of the inhabitants.*

Left: A theatre poster of 1857 features various members of the Yelland and Wickham families who were well-known amateur performers. The 'Theatre Royal' was probably the temporarily renamed Assembly Rooms in the town. (PC)

Below: Another poster from two years later which again features members of the Yelland family who, on this occasion, were performing in Appledore. A manuscript section attached to the back of this poster apologises for the lack of scenery and backdrops. (PC)

Above: *A fascinating photograph of the local cyclists' club on the Quay, c.1900. Everyone is wearing a hat, the trees on the Quay are spindly and the lady cyclist and her partner look both uncomfortable and unsafe.* (AB)

Right: *A formidable-looking group of young men belonging to Bideford Football Club in around 1890 – at a time when football actually meant rugby.* (PC)

The Bideford Cycling Club photographed in the 1930s on one of their runs out to the Yeo Valley. (PU)

W.H. Short, Mayor in 1950, can be seen presenting the thanks of the borough to Mr Burton, the co-founder of the Burton Art Gallery. Note the town clerk in his wig below the dais. (PC)

The Burton Art Gallery was opened as a memorial to Mary Burton by her father Thomas and his friend Hubert Coop. This photograph from July 1951 shows construction being carried out. (NDJ)

The money raised went to the construction of New Road. Not all amateurs were met with the rapturous applause accorded Handford's Company. In 1871 the local paper reviewed a performance by the Bideford Amateur Dramatic Club:

The acting was bad, very bad; the provincialisms were glaring; and when we add to this the fact that the prompter's services were continually required and that his voice was heard in all parts of the room, it is not too much to say that the apparent neglect of the members in regard to the not very laborious parts in the simple pieces selected for performance was culpable in the extreme.

In the 1860s there were frequent 'assemblies and balls, concerts and performances... at the Assembly Rooms and Town Hall.' Performers included 'Ethiopian Serenaders', a troupe of dwarves and a hypnotist. In 1869, £2,670 having been raised in £5 shares, the Music Hall in Bridgeland Street was opened to replace the Mansion House. The main hall held 600 people and rapidly became the centre for entertainment in Bideford, staging musical shows, plays and other amusements. Travelling theatres also visited the town, usually pitching their tents on the riverbank near the Pill. Puritanism still lingered in Bideford, for in 1882, one of these shows was denounced in the local press, because 'much evil results from the indiscriminate congregation of young people at the performances,' this being 'highly dangerous to the moral and social principles of the inhabitants of the town.' Most of the Town Council, however, thought this exaggerated and said it would be 'unfair to take away from poor people one of their few means of amusement, whilst those better off retain the privilege of going to higher-class theatres.'

Earlier, a public meeting in November 1845 had led to the setting up of the Bideford Literary and Scientific Institute – 'a great means of diffusing knowledge, and for arousing into healthy action the

dormant mental powers,' according to the first lecturer. Within five years membership had grown to 100 men – and two women. Meetings were held in the Mansion House until 1851, when they moved to Mr Lee's in High Street (the site of New Look in 2004). After an unfortunate squabble between churchmen and nonconformists on the committee, the Institute disappeared, but later rose phoenix-like as the Bideford Improvement Society. To give working people an equal chance of 'improvement', the Bideford Mechanics' Institute was founded in November 1854 'on liberal principles'. Charles Kingsley, who was a Christian Socialist, gave the first lecture.

In 1877, when the town's first public library was opened, it was hoped that as:

... a place of resort for apprentices and young men, after leaving their shops and their counting houses, it would not only prevent them to a certain extent from getting in to evil company, but would be a resort for relaxation and recreation, which would benefit them morally, intellectually and physically.

After five years in what is now the Masonic Hall in Bridgeland Street, the library was moved to Bridge Buildings, and in 1906 came to rest where it remains at the time of writing, in buildings erected by the Carnegie Trust. In 1908, as an extension to the library, Inkerman Rogers, a watchmaker and self-taught local historian, set up a museum, but it was dispersed many years ago. There is, however, an art gallery, given by Thomas Burton in memory of his daughter Mary (1904–49), some of whose drawings it contains. Burton, a Londoner who became a businessman, lay preacher and Mayor in Bideford, was joined in this venture by Hubert Coop, who gave paintings, drawings and other items. The gallery has attracted other gifts, is the centre for a society of local artists and, following enhancements in 1999 and 2003, provides a better art exhibition space and a museum section.

The new swings being erected in Victoria Park in October 1952. (NDJ)

Youth organisations have always been important in Bideford. The local Boy Scouts are seen here opening their HQ in June 1952. (NDJ)

BOROUGH OF BIDEFORD

OPENING OF
KING GEORGE'S FIELD
BY
HIS ROYAL HIGHNESS
THE DUKE OF EDINBURGH, K.G.

29th October, 1952

OFFICIAL PROGRAMME

Left: *Following the Second World War Bideford decided to upgrade its park facilities and was honoured with the presence of the Duke of Edinburgh, who opened the new northern part of the park – as commemorated in this souvenir programme.* (PC)

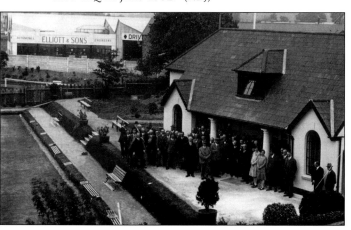

Above right: *The Chingswell Street bowling club at the opening of its new clubhouse. Elliott's Garage at the rear is still in existence in 2005, although much changed from the structure seen here.*

Below: *An early photograph of the bowling-green at the bottom of Willet Street. At the time of writing it is on a site a little farther to the east.* (NDMT)

The Palace Cinema in Bridgeland Street had its façade updated after the First World War, but this wasn't enough to prevent its closure in 1959. (AB)

The Strand Cinema was opened in 1939 to hold 816 customers. This shot from 1953 highlights its very attractive setting. The building was demolished in the 1980s and, after some years as a car park, a block of flats was built on the site. (PC)

'Moving pictures' were first shown in 1896 in a tent on the Strand, and the Bijou Theatre Cinema opened before 1914 in what is, at the time of writing, a night-club in Lower Gunstone. Another cinema (which also had live shows) was the Palladium, opened just after the First World War. Its main auditorium still exists behind Patt's fruit shop in Mill Street. As people's tastes changed, the Music Hall itself began to show films, and eventually became the Palace Cinema. It closed in 1959 but its rival, the Strand Cinema, survived it for over 20 years. It was opened in 1939 and soon became a haven of refuge for Jewish refugees from Poland and Czechoslovakia who were housed in tents on the Sports Ground behind the cinema. To pass the time before they were called on to serve in the Pioneer Corps, they formed a group of instrumentalists. Some of the professional musicians kept in touch and became the nucleus of the famous post-war Philharmonic Orchestra. The cinema itself was knocked down and replaced with a rather overbearing block of flats designed for older residents.

The ten archers, recorded in the muster of 'able men' in Bideford in 1569, practised (perhaps in Buttgarden), not for sport, but as a military duty. For pastime, the 'Bowlinge Alley' at Nunnery (near where the police station is situated in 2004) may have already

The new gates to Victoria Park were opened on 9 November 1912. (PS)

been in use. In the eighteenth century a new bowling-green was laid out at the other end of the town next to the Bath Garden where, before 1768, William Hamlyn Heywood, a local surgeon, had 'erected and built a convenient Bathing and Dressing Room' on the bank of the Pill. He would have been promoting a salt-water cure rather than sport, but the attempt to turn Bideford into a watering place is interesting.

Rowing was a necessary skill for many Bidefordians, but people also enjoyed races, and Bideford Regatta was well-established by the mid-nineteenth century. In 1858 one of Heard's emigrant ships moored beside the Quay was used as a committee boat, making an elegant backdrop for the proceedings on the river. Water carnivals were also held, often after dark, with lantern-lit floats.

By the end of the nineteenth century, local clubs provided opportunities for amateur athletics, cricket, football, bowling, tennis and cycling, and before the First World War there were also clubs for rowing, photography, hockey and swimming. Many sports clubs used the facilities of Victoria Park, opened in 1912 and greatly extended in 1952. The interwar years before the advent of television were the heyday of local societies, and by the 1930s even more clubs existed, including amateur dramatics, rugby, Scouts, Guides, a girls' club, British Legion, chess, Church Lads' Brigade, and Toc H. There were also gun and rifle clubs, and societies for fanciers of almost anything – from cage birds to heavy horses!

A group with a long history in the town are the Freemasons. They first appeared in 1775 when a lodge that had formed 12 years earlier in Appledore moved to the town. It only lasted two years although a new one called 'The Good Intention' was formed in 1783 but was superseded nine years later by 'The Faithful Lodge', which met on the Quay in the Newfoundland Inn. This disappeared in 1823 but in 1843 the fourth (and continuing) lodge formed. Known as 'Benevolence', at the time of writing it is based in Bridgeland Street where it has been since October 1875.

The largest shows ever staged in Bideford marked the widening of the bridge in 1925 and the opening of Kingsley Road in 1927, along with the coronation of George VI ten years later. All took the form of historical pageants, with hundreds of townspeople re-enacting scenes from the town's past. The Garden Theatre, opened in 1934 on the Pill, staged a wide selection of shows, dances and entertainments. In this building, which in 2004 is the subject of rebuilding plans, Paul Scofield had an early taste of repertory theatre. Other notable performers to appear in the town have included Benjamin Britten and Peter Pears, Humphrey Littleton, and A.G. Street, all in the Taw and Torridge Festival of the Arts in 1955, which presented orchestral music, jazz, lectures, plays and fireworks.

Although television and video have sounded the death knell of the cinema and much self-created entertainment, they have promoted other sports; snooker is popular, for instance, and most pubs provide darts or other games. Street entertainments take place at Christmas and New Year, summer fun runs start on the Quay, a purpose-built drama and music complex has been opened at the comprehensive school and a new theatre at Edgehill College. A new and very well-used skateboard park at Bank End has been provided by the Bridge Trust and Torridge District Council and a new sports ground has been opened at East-the-Water. At the time of writing, plans are also in hand for a new Multi Use Games Area somewhere in the town. Tomorrow's Bidefordians will have leisure opportunities undreamed of by their ancestors.

Above: *Vast crowds were attracted to the 1925 Pageant in the Sports Ground and a portion is shown here in front of the old stand.* (PC)

Above right: *A street party in New Street in the mid-1930s to mark some royal occasion. The picture includes: Joe Keen, Trevor Slade, ? Headon, Teddie Headon, Albert Blackmore, Rosie Graham, Flossie Hopkins, Doris Schiller, Maud Cole, ? Patt, Marjorie Braddick, ? Cole, Jack Schiller, ? Cole, ? Little, Mrs Kent, Mrs Little, Bessie Fowler, Maud Sherborne, 'Granny' Cole.* (MS)

Below: *This is thought to be the Bideford Carnival or Pageant of 1937 processing along the Quay.* (PU)

Below: *Bidefordians took every chance to party and here we see a group of local children celebrating a royal occasion in the 1930s in New Street. The street was a bustling and friendly place but was demolished in the so-called 'slum' clearances of the 1950s. New houses were only built on the site in 1988.* (MS)

EAST-THE-WATER COMMUNITY ASSOCIATION
(Chairman : F. W. BEER, Esq.)
Presents

" BEATING THE CLOCK ! "

Photo   S. J. Turner

BRIDGE RUN

THURSDAY, JUNE 1st, 1950

8 p.m.   LENGTH OF COURSE 225 Yds.

FOR A PERPETUAL TROPHY PRESENTED BY
MR. AND MRS. F. W. BEER

Convenor and Referee –   –   –   T. Taylor
Starting Judges   –   F. Mayne, A. Bond
Judges, Winning Post -   K. Parsons, A. Pridham
Clock Stewards   –   –   W. Beer, J. Down
Timekeepers - E. J. Northwood, F. V. Cole

Souvenir Programme -   - 3d.

Above: *Boat trips were very popular and here we see happy tourists posing in the* Hobah *of Bideford, c.1920, before it set off down the Torridge.* (PU)

Right: *The front of a programme advertising the 'Bridge Run' in 1950. The aim of this was to get across the bridge before the church clock struck all eight chimes. On this occasion the four runners were W. Vickery, R. Hockaday, R. Barrett and E. May.* (PC)

THE LANDING OF THE PILGRIM FATHERS

Left: *A float from what is thought to be the Bideford Carnival or Pageant of 1937, on the Pill.* (PU)

Right: *A 1950 carnival float at East-the-Water. Left to right:* Wally Waterhouse, Basil Pidgeon and Reggie Denford. (BP)

OPENING
OF THE
New Bideford-Northam Road
By the Mayor of Bideford,
Alderman J. M. METHERELL, J.P., C.A.
AND
The Chairman of Northam Urban District
Council,
Major-General Sir J. MURRAY IRWIN,
K.C.M.G., C.B.
ON
Whit-Monday, 6th June, 1927

PROGRAMME
OF
GREAT PAGEANT
Of Local History and Romance
AND
OFFICIAL GUIDE
OF DAY'S PROCEEDINGS.
6d.

ADMISSION to Sports Ground, 1/- ; Reserved Seats
Grand Stand, 5/- ; Unreserved and Enclosure, 3/6 ;
Children, Half-price.

"Bideford Gazette," Ltd., Printers.

Above, right and below right: Bideford Carnival still takes place annually at the start of the twenty-first century. These views are taken from various carnivals of the 1950s – before the influence of television became all-pervading. (NDJ)

Above: *The front page of the progamme for a 'Great Pageant Of Local History and Romance', held to mark the opening of Kingsley Road, 1927.* (PC)

Left: *A group of 'walking' characters from the 1937 carnival.* (PU)

Chapter 9

The Bridge Trust

Inseparable from the history of Bideford is the Bridge Trust. No one knows when the Trust began but it must have been some time after the construction of the bridge in the thirteenth century. Very little is known about the early Trust – there is a list of its members from the 1550s and a Chancery Court case from 1608. What seems clear is that rich Bidefordians left property to the Trust in order to give it an income to be spent on repairs to the bridge, and over the years, with additional purchases, the Trust has become Bideford's biggest landlords if we exclude council-owned housing.

Detailed knowledge of the Trust and its workings dates from 1764, the year from which the first surviving minutes survive. At this date there appear to have been some 15 trustees, or feoffees as they were then called. Most were merchants or gentlemen, although a few clergymen and service personnel appear in later lists. Then, as in the twenty-first century, the Trust was a self-perpetuating oligarchy with members choosing whom they wanted to fill up empty places. Thus in August 1773, for example, eight surviving feoffees met to choose seven new members from a list of ten hopefuls. In 2005 there are 12 trustees consisting of eight laymen, three representatives from the Town Council and the Mayor of the day.

The Trust has always employed a solicitor as its steward to handle its legal affairs and he has been helped by one or more wardens who have charge of property maintenance. Meetings are held at the time of writing in a room in one of the Trust's properties in Bridgeland Street, but in the past they were held in a room in the old Town Hall (where Bridge Buildings stand at the time of writing).

Following the collapse of two arches in 1968 ownership of the bridge passed to the Ministry of Transport, but prior to that the Trust spent much time and money on the structure. The bridge's early history has been dealt with in Chapter Two, but from the minutes we can see just how much effort went into the upkeep of the structure. From the earliest days regular inspections were carried out along with regular repairs. In 1788, for example, the warden was ordered to 'repave' 60 feet of the bridge with local stone, whilst in 1791 the feoffees were writing to a Mr Stevens pointing out that a wagon of his had recently crossed the bridge so heavily laden 'as they think will injure the… Bridge.' In 1793 we get a rare glimpse of a long-vanished part of the bridge when Bartholomew Ward and Thomas Burnard were charged a guinea each for 'the Damage done to the Cross of the Bridge.' This cross is clearly shown in a near-contemporary engraving of the bridge. It seems to have been a long-lived feature as it was almost certainly the source of the odd mistake on the town seal, which shows a masted vessel sailing through one of the arches with what appears to be part of its mast showing above the parapets – the engraver having elided the mast and cross together.

The year 1794 saw the first major enlargement of the bridge when Edward Kendal widened the three central arches 'according to the Plan recommended by Captain Darcey.' Not content with undertaking improvements to the arches the feoffees also purchased some stables in East-the-Water in order to

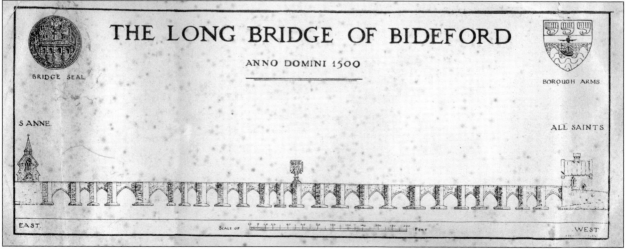

Donn's carefully measured drawing of the bridge was published in the Gentleman's Magazine *in July 1751 and clearly shows the different widths of each arch.* (NDA)

demolish them and 'Render the Access to the Bridge more Commodious.' The slower pace of life in those days is clearly shown by the fact that it took Kendal a year to produce his detailed plans 'for widening the Four Arches of the Bridge... Two feet each side.' The contract was extremely simple in that Kendal was to be paid £295 altogether made up of three tranches viz: £100 when the 'Centers & materials are provided', another £100 'when the work is one half done' and the rest when the job was completed. For his part he agreed to forfeit all the money if any of his work 'gives way' within seven years of its completion – as well as making good any repairs that would then be required.

Once started Kendal seems to have worked rapidly as his first-stage payment was paid within four months of signing the contract, along with another £6.6.0. for 'Flagging that new part of the Bridge now widened, of both sides, Eighteen Inches of each sides.' Evidently the feoffees were more than satisfied with the work as in August 1795 they agreed to pay Kendal another £140 to widen another two arches. As the final flourish to their newly widened bridge the feoffees ordered the steward to purchase eight lamps to be placed along the structure and adjoining Quay.

All went well until 1802 when a contemporary note in the minutes records that:

Whereas some malicious persons have repeatedly thrown down the Coping Stones of the Bridge & otherwise damaged the same; it is ordered that Two persons should be from this Day appointed at the expence of the Bridge Stock to keep watch in the Watch House of the said Bridge in the night Season in order to detect the Offender or Offenders.

A new 'Centry Box' was to be erected for these watchmen and two extra lamps were also ordered.

Five years later in March 1807 the feoffees decided to undertake a second major building scheme. The minutes record that the members 'Resolved in our Opinion it will be a public benefit if the Long Bridge was widened throughout in the same manner as the Six Arches in the Middle.' Advertisements were placed in some unnamed newspapers inviting tenders to widen four arches 'nearest to the Town from the arches already widened.' Within just three weeks six tenders were received, although interestingly Kendal, who had carried out the previous widening, was not among them. The contract took a little negotiating but on June 29 of that year Rowland Moase agreed to widen five arches at £50 per arch within four months under a penalty clause of £200. He also agreed to keep the work in repair for seven years at his own expense. The feoffees further contracted with him to take down and rebuild as many of the cutwaters at the base of the piers as they saw fit for 10s. each.

Moase's work must have been satisfactory as we find the feoffees paying him £106.4s.4d. in December 1808 for widening nine arches, rather than the five they agreed. At the same meeting, however, it was noted that the Trust was to repay £213.12s.0d. due 'to the Bideford Bank for money borrowed for widening the said five Arches,' which suggests the reference to nine might be a clerical error. Whatever the truth of the matter Moase was employed again in 1809 to clear two arches of the bridge which had become blocked with debris. As he was paid £10 for this it suggests the job was fairly large and probably involved some form of dredging.

A month later, in September 1809, the feoffees noted that they had resolved to widen the remaining arches of the bridge the next year, following publication of an invitation to tender in 'the Exeter paper'. It was also noted that they would obtain estimates for 'throwing two Arches into one' if it could be carried out safely. Presumably this was to avoid blockages in the narrower archways.

Not content with this major scheme, in November of the same year the feoffees were discussing a plan to construct a drawbridge at the eastern end of the bridge. One assumes this was to allow the passage of large boats at all states of the tide. After due consideration, however, the idea was shelved and two arches on the eastern side of the bridge were chosen to be 'thrown into one' in order to aid navigation. Also at this meeting it was decided to enlarge all the individual arches and the minutes record in detail the method of construction and the materials to be used.

Once the news got out, however, one aspect of the scheme seems to have caused some local concern as it was noted that a public meeting was to be held in the Bridge Hall where 'the Commercial Inhabitants [were to] be invited to attend to reconsider the matter' – this being the plan to combine two arches into one. The meeting decided that the scheme 'would be highly disadvantageous to the Trade of Bideford,' and so it was dropped.

Meanwhile, two tenders had been received for widening the arches and although Moase had submitted one he lost out to James Green who was described as a civil engineer of Exeter. His first detailed survey of the bridge revealed that the parapet walls were so irregular that they couldn't be made uniform and that demolition was the only option. The new parapet was to be some three feet nine inches high and to include 'an inscription in the Parapet'. What this might have been has unfortunately not been recorded. As well as widening the arches Green also agreed to 'reduce the recesses in the parapet walls over the Piers to an hexagonal form.' These recesses were to allow people to shelter as coaches drove across the still-narrow bridge and were very necessary at this date. The cost of all this construction work was put at £1,240 and a completion date of December 1810 was set. Some £1,000 was to be raised by the sale of the Trust's stock holdings. Further surveys, however, revealed problems with

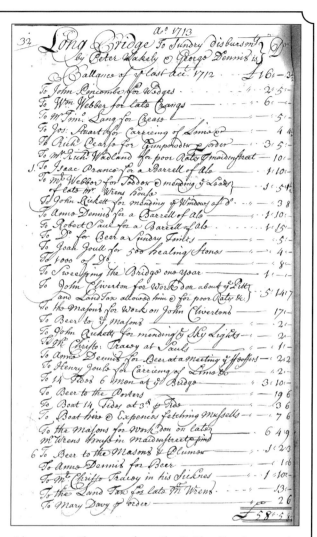

Above: *A page from the Bridge Trust accounts for 1689. Drawn up by John Barnes and Tristram Dennis, it shows payments for 'Windless' or stakes used to protect the base of the bridge's piers, as well as 2d. for 'Nailes and a Cay [key] for Watch house'. This was put up on the bridge to help stop vandalism.* (NDRO)

Above: *Another page from the Bridge Trust accounts, this time from 1713. Drawn up by Peter Wakely and George Dennis, payments for a 'Barrell of Ale' feature several times. Note also the payment of 7s.6d. for 'fetching Mussells'. These were placed on the sterlings around the bases of the pillars to help protect the bridge against scouring.* (NDRO)

Below: *A postcard sent to a soldier serving in India in the 6th Battalion Devon Regiment in 1914. The card shows very clearly the iron parapets put in place in the 1864–66 widening. The message reads 'Just to remind you of the dear old homestead. Fond love, Glad'.* (PC)

Above: *In 1917 the government requisitioned the rolling stock of the Bideford, Westward Ho! and Appledore Railway and a temporary line was laid across the bridge to allow its movement to the main line.* (PC)

Right: *During the reconstruction an oil lorry driven by Charles Cloke crashed over the bridge and, although seriously injured, Cloke survived.*

Above: *A striking shot from February 1954 clearly showing the bases of the bridge pillars which acted to prevent scouring.* (PC)

Left: *This shot shows how thin the supporting column became in 1968.* (AB)

Below: *A dramatic photograph from January 1968 of the two collapsed arches of Bideford bridge. Their collapse led to the severance of the two halves of the town and a massive traffic diversion for many months before the bridge was repaired and reopened.* (PC)

Above: *The bridge in February 1895 when the Torridge froze over.* (AB)

Right: *Another shot of ice on the Torridge, this time from January 1963. It is thought frost damage associated with some cold winters helped weaken the bridge before the arches collapsed in 1968.* (PC)

Below: *Work going on to rebuild and strengthen the collapsed arches of the bridge in 1968. The temporary footbridge can clearly be seen.* (PC)

A close-up of the footbridge before it was put in place. (PC)

The footbridge just prior to being lowered in place. (PC)

the defensive wickerwork surrounding one of the piers and one of the cutwaters. This extra cost was added to the revised specification where top-quality Penarth Ashlar stone was to be used instead of 'common' stone – a decision which added £760 to the overall cost and raised it to £2,000.

Further additional costs were involved when, in December, the feoffees decided to repair the footways and to re-pave the 'Horseway' on the bridge. The stone in this instance came from Orchard Hill, just outside Bideford (the quarry still remains at the time of writing). This added £466 to the overall bill and forced the feoffees to borrow £100, as they did not have adequate funds to cover Green's bill. That even this wasn't enough is shown when in March 1811 the feoffees had to borrow another £700 to cover their costs, although the eventual bill for paving only came to £300. With further alterations to the eastern end of the bridge, work was only apparently completed in November 1811, although Green did not get his final payment until February 1812 and the debts incurred by the Trust were only finally cleared six years later.

Within a few months of the completion of Green's work, however, vandals had broken 'the corner Stone forming the Tablet on the Centre of the Bridge.' Presumably the watchmen hired in 1802 had been discontinued and this time the feoffees chose to have handbills printed and distributed, and two notices posted at each end of the bridge offering a reward of ten guineas for the capture and conviction of those responsible. These measures had to be repeated in 1816, although only five guineas were offered on this occasion.

This vandalism was minor when compared with the occasion in 1815 when Captain Jones, master of the *Britannia*, and Captain Barrett, master of the *Thomas and Eliza*, had through their 'carelessness or Negligence' with their vessels made 'breaches' in 'the Walls of the Bridge'. They were charged the cost of

repairs and the feoffees noted that if such damage occurred again those responsible would be charged double the costs of the repairs required – a decision made known to the local shipmasters by the printing of '100 Notices to this Effect'. That this was not an idle threat is shown in 1820, when Samuel Cooke was being pursued for damages done to the bridge when his vessel collided with it.

Everyday wear and tear was probably more damaging than the occasional vandal or careless shipmaster. Certainly in 1818, only seven years after its last major resurfacing, the feoffees had to re-pave the whole bridge. To keep costs down they chose to use 'Stones to be found in the River Torridge', whilst in 1821 re-paving was being done 'with the Stones in Front of the Prison.' Only two years later re-paving was required again, and this time the feoffees ordered the existing surface to be broken up and concerted into a road 'on the Plan of Mr McAdam'. The famous engineer was asked to supervise the work but, as a later reference in the same year makes clear, the pavement was actually only repaired, and thus McAdam probably never worked in Bideford.

Many writers have commented on the chapels said to have been associated with the bridge. One definite reference to a chapel occurs in 1821, when Mrs Mary Wilcock added one life to her lease of 'the Chapple and Toll House' at East-the-Water for £10. No notice of this chapel actually operating as a religious building exists in the Trust's minutes, so we must assume it had lost its original function by this date. A later reference seems to indicate that the chapel had been incorporated into a shop.

All this work must have secured the structural stability of the old bridge and, following this, the feoffees turned their attention to more detailed but equally important matters. In December 1826 'The

Propriety of Lighting the Bridge was taken into Consideration' and, following agreement that such a course was 'highly desirable', a committee was set up to prepare a report on its costs and implications. Presumably the earlier lamps had become decrepit. The following December, after tenders had been sought, Philip Tardrew agreed to erect 12 lamps on the bridge at a cost of up to £60. The lamps were probably oil fuelled and would have been of great benefit to the town, which perhaps explains why the then large sum of ten guineas was offered as a reward to capture 'some evil disposed person or persons' who damaged one of the lamps in December 1828. Two of the lamps were stolen in 1832 and another reward, this time for £5, was offered for information. By 1835 or 1836 these lamps had been replaced with gas-burning ones which gave a much brighter light.

In 1829 the bridge wardens reported that the 'Watteling around the bottom of the Piers' of the bridge was decaying and needed to be replaced. Various engineers were consulted, including the noted Mr Telford who declined the job. That the job was complex can be seen in the reference where the steward was ordered to 'provide the necessary instruments for driving the Piles to protect the foundation of the Bridge.' These piles were to be between six and seven inches thick and a mix of new wood and 'Old Ship Timber' was to be used. A later reference in 1836 proves that this job was ongoing, as the feoffees gave instructions to prepare piles from elm trees blown down 'during the late gales' and keep them in reserve for when they were needed.

Only basic maintenance was carried out for the next decade or so and it was only in 1841 that the steward requested the employment of an engineer from Plymouth to inspect 'the Stakes and Freathing' under the bridge, as they needed large-scale restoration. Whether he was consulted or not is unclear but the next year saw the feoffees calling for the necessary repairs to be done as soon as possible. The detailed costs of the work are noted in the minutes. Following these works, which appear to have taken longer than expected, the bridge warden was ordered to prepare monthly reports on the state of the bridge from 'personal Examination'. With the railway boom of the 1840s it was inevitable that a rail company would apply to run a rail across the bridge – and in 1846 three companies were given permission, but nothing ever happened. Indeed the only railway to cross the structure was in 1917 when the engines of the Bideford, Westward Ho! and Appledore Railway were taken across a temporary line on their way to France to help the war effort. The railway may not have led to any changes but in 1853 the Trust met with the Town Council to discuss widening the bridge. After innumerable false starts, and counter-plans to build a 'light Bridge' at Cleave Houses in Northam, the widening was completed in 1866. This

When the bridge arches collapsed in 1968, Bidefordians were ferried across the river in small boats. (CB)

extended the width from nine feet to 14 feet nine inches and replaced the ancient stone parapets with steel ones. A further widening scheme was considered 33 years later but was not carried out until 1925, when the roadway was extended to its present 16 feet. Also at this time the steel parapets were taken down and the reinforced stone ones, still extant at the time of writing, were built.

The newly widened and strengthened bridge continued to serve the town well both as a link between its two halves and also as a tourist attraction – as the multitude of picture postcards over the years show. Tourism, however, halted in 1939 with the outbreak of war, and over the next six years the bridge was guarded by the Bideford Home Guard against possible enemy attack. Its importance as a transport link in the West Country was endorsed with the discovery of German 'Invasion Plan' maps , which clearly showed how interested the Wehrmacht would have been in its capture, had they invaded. During this period exceptionally heavy military loads, notably United States Army tank transporters, crossed the bridge, one weighing all of 120 tons.

The bridge escaped damage but from 1945 onwards traffic rapidly increased both in weight and numbers and the trustees became worried about the amount of wear and tear the bridge was suffering. In 1967 large cracks in the masonry were repaired, but on 9 January 1968 the two westerly arches collapsed. The bridge was closed and enormous disruption ensued. Described as 'the greatest local calamity since the plague of 1646,' a passenger ferry had to be organised to link the two parts of the town before a temporary footbridge was put in place. Repairs took many months with ownership passing to the Ministry of Transport.

In 2000, doubts were first aired by the Town Council as to the safety of the bridge and were soon found to be justified. In 2002 various options for the future of the bridge were put forward, but at the time of writing it is still uncertain which will go ahead.

Although upkeep of the bridge swallowed up most of the Trust's funds, surplus money has been spent on helping Bideford and its people. The first

A view of Bridgeland Street with the town council, constables and band parading down it on an occasion, c.1900. (PC)

record we have of this is the building and opening up of Bridgeland Street in the late-seventeenth century. This development replaced a jumble of old houses and riverside yards and was so successful that in around 1704 Daniel Defoe wrote that the street was as:

> ... broad as the High Street of Exeter, well-built, and which is more than all, well inhabited, with considerable and wealthy merchants, who trade to most parts of the trading world.

Soon afterwards the feoffees constructed almshouses in Meddon Street which, in 1738, became Bideford's first workhouse. In 1742, a year of excessive mortality, the Trust gave a plot of land some 60 yards square to the town as an 'overspill' graveyard, the one around St Mary's being uncomfortably full. This was at the corner of Honestone Street and Old Town and still exists at the time of writing as part of Old Town Cemetery, which in its turn was given to the town by the Trust in 1842.

Around 1758 the Trust constructed the original Bridge Buildings on a site at the end of the bridge. This housed the Trust's meeting room, the Grammar School, the Town Hall, a wine cellar and even had the stocks set up in front of it (they are in the Burton Art Gallery and Museum at the time of writing).

In 1761, as noted elsewhere, the feoffees purchased the Fox and Goose public house on the Quay and turned it into the 'Mansion House' for the Mayor. In the mid-nineteenth century they gave a site in the High Street for the erection of a Post Office (the site where Lloyds TSB was in 2004), whilst in 1882 the old Bridge Buildings were replaced with the ones still there in 2004. This massive new structure housed the Bideford Library and School of Art for some years before they were moved to other locations. Building operations cost some £4,500 and virtually bankrupted the Trust – although it was noted at the opening that Bideford was the smallest town in Britain to have its own library.

In the twentieth century the Trust refurbished the old Friendship Café opposite the Pannier Market, along with redeveloping Post Office Mews into a charming area of town houses. Many other smaller schemes have been carried out and the Trust rarely has any trouble finding tenants for its buildings, owing to its very high reputation as a caring and fair landlord.

Other spare funds have supported many charitable undertakings. For many years in the eighteenth and nineteenth centuries the Trust gave £10 a year to the town's poor who were 'worthy of such Charity'. In years of exceptional hardship this was increased, so that in 1767 some £90, a huge sum at that time, was spent on buying wheat and selling it to the poor at a subsidised price. In 1800 £40 worth of soup was distributed through the town, whilst in 1831 the feoffees leased two acres of land in 'North Down Lane' as allotments 'for the Occupation and Employment of the Industrious Poor.'

More unusually the Trust minutes record that on five occasions between 1787 and 1801 it was 'Ordered that the Poor People of the parish be inoculated at the Expense of the Bridge at five shillings each to be done jointly by the Surgeons of the Town.' This was probably as a preventative measure against smallpox, which left sufferers badly disfigured if they actually managed to survive. The Trust has also been responsible for providing the town's fire engines, its prison (in 1731) and a 'good bowling green' (in the 1720s), as well as supporting a wide range of educational establishments in the town as detailed in Chapter 13. In the early-twenty-first century the Trust gives book grants and bursaries to Bidefordians undertaking university courses and provides 'Start Up' grants to would-be businessmen and women. In addition they provide much-needed funding to many local organisations and sports clubs. Clearly Bideford is lucky to have the Bridge Trust.

The uniformed staff line up outside the Post Office in High Street, c.1900. The large opening to the left allowed the mail coaches to reach a yard at the rear. In 2004 the site houses the Lloyds TSB bank and its owner, the Bridge Trust, recently replaced the old clock which had long disappeared. (PC)

Chapter 10

The Town Council

Running in parallel with the Trust has been the Town Council, or Corporation as it was known in earlier years. The body was set up in 1574 and sadly its early records are lost. For many years, however, we know it was run by a tightly-knit group of often-related gentlemen and merchants. Records survive in some numbers from the eighteenth century but it seemed to do little other than meet occasionally and feast regularly. If it was not corrupt it was hardly dynamic, and when it was swept away in the changes following the Municipal Reform Act in 1830 it was probably the best thing that could have happened for Bideford.

As part of the events leading up to the passing of the Act, Parliament collected information on the state of every borough in England and Wales. The government-appointed inspector visited Bideford on 5 December 1833 and his report fills four foolscap printed pages and reveals a wealth of information on how the town had been run for most of the eighteenth and the opening years of the nineteenth centuries.

The Corporation consisted of a Mayor, eight aldermen (including the Mayor) and ten capital burgesses or leading townsmen. This body employed a recorder (or solicitor), a town clerk, a coroner, two serjeants-at-mace (rate collectors) 16 constables (generally elected annually from the towns-people), a chief constable, a beadle or town crier, a clerk of the market, surveyors of weights and measures, a receiver of assize returns (a type of trading standards officer) and a gaoler. The Mayor was elected each year on 21 September and received an allowance of £20 per year,

Reuben Clements of 3 Myrtle Grove who died in 1948 aged 90. He was a postman who served as Macebearer and Beadle for many years. (PC)

although it was noted that 'The Mayor's allowance never covers his expenditure; the difference is made up by himself.' At the inquiry date Thomas Burnard, a 40-year-old merchant, was the chief citizen. Both the aldermen and town clerk were appointed for life and this could obviously lead to corruption and secrecy. Oddly, the clerk received no salary, but he could raise his own income through various means. At the time of the inquiry the clerk was Charles Carter junr and his 'emoluments', as they are euphemistically termed, were put at £60 per annum.

Of the Corporation's employees the main one was the gaoler who doubled up as the Governor of the Workhouse – for which posts he was paid £20 a year and had a house in which to live. His gaol had been 'fitted up' around 1831 and contained six cells with 'boarded floors and glazed windows'. It was located in what is the Royal Hotel in 2005, where several of the cells still exist. Prisoners were kept locked up for most of the time, there being no exercise yard, just 'a narrow passage under the level of the ground' where they could stretch their legs. There were never that many prisoners as the untrained, and often unwilling, elected constables did not regularly patrol the town but were only called out in times of emergency. The report notes that 'The town is stated to be peaceable and the Police sufficient.'

Intriguingly the town does not appear to have suffered the political battles that often erupted in Barnstaple. As the report puts it:

From the circumstances of Bideford not returning members to Parliament, party spirit does not seem to have run so high in this as in the other south-western boroughs.

Indeed 'The corporation and inhabitants appear to be on good terms, and the former are anxious to employ their small resource for the benefit of the town.'

Bideford Town Council dates from 1836 when the first elections were held under the system of wider suffrage – although the number of voters was still small. Only one of the candidates stood under a political label, as a Conservative, but he came bottom of the poll. Political affiliations were not always stated although membership of either the Conservative Club (founded 1895 in Bridgeland Street) or the Liberal Club (founded 1899 in High Street) made clear a councillor's allegiance. In 1967 two would-be councillors stood as Liberals and since then political labels have been used. In 2004 the town's council is split between Liberal Democrats, Community Alliance, Independents and the Green Party.

The council has always had two main responsibilities; to raise money via rates and to spend it for

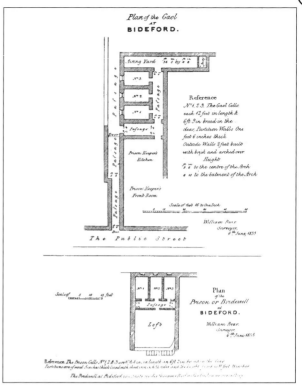

The 1833 report into the state of local government in Bideford was accompanied by this map showing the borough limits. Note the small extent of East-the-Water and the width of the Pill stream. (PC)

Plans of the old Bideford Gaol (part of the Royal Hotel at the time of writing) and the Bridewell in Meddon Street from 1835. At this date John Pim looked after both for £10 per year. (PC)

A magnificent shot of the Edwardian Town Council in full session in the Town Hall. The nature of the occasion was not recorded. (PC)

Right: *This very old-looking chemist's shop was at the junction of High and Grenville Streets where a café stands in 2004. The owner, Joce, was the gentleman about whom the election poem (below) was written. Joce manufactured a special soft drink from secret ingredients and water from a well under his shop.* (BL)

ALLITERATION.

ANTECEDENT TO 1st NOVEMBER, 1855.

BIDEFORD.

VOTE FOR JOCE! VOTE FOR JOCE!

Is placarded in words verbose!
To be a COUNCILMAN! suppose,
In lieu of one become abstruse.—

VOTE FOR JOCE! VOTE FOR JOCE!

Is now the all-prevailing news!
A Townsman genuine and spruce,
Gentlemen wish to introduce,
To Aldermen and Mr. Buse,
And other Councillors, of cou'se,
To have a Seat with them!—propose
Measures for good Town governing laws!

If ill from eating duck or goose,
Or any animal more gross,
He'll cure you with a gratis dose,
Of old cognac, or vineyard juice,
Even if occasion'd bellicose;
Then recommend your eating ' puss.'—

VOTE FOR JOCE! VOTE FOR JOCE!

Responding voters cry, " here goes!"
This opportunity I sha'nt lose,
If I go to vote in working clothes;
Bad-luck to him that does refuse,
And may he dye within his shoes.

VOTE FOR JOCE! VOTE FOR JOCE!

The universal motto, prose,
Confronts the gazer's precious nose,
Against the wall behind the rose,
Wherever one may seek repose,
Bedeck'd with donkey or jim crows.

VOTE FOR JOCE! VOTE FOR JOCE!—

Who is this gentleman? of cou'se—
The stranger asks. To be joeose,
Old Esculapius says, ' he knows,'
That he sells liniment for blows—
Obtain'd in an election cause,
And renders Cotty's oils for jaws
That have been scratch'd by lady-claws,
Pesill'cam plaster for sore toes,
And chemicals, all apropo's;
Not stuffs for such—malt-liquor brews,
To save the hops,—no! none of those.
Drugs from Apothecary's Hall,—aloes,
And patent medicines from Soho's!

Genuine seeds for him that sows,
For flowers red or white as snows,
That in the bower blooms and blows,
Its fragrance all around that throws,
Parterres for Ladies to compose,
Or cottage exhibition shows;

Those seed that in the meadow grows,
That waves when ripe like tide that flows,
Those sown for fodder or milch cows,
Or arish lands where cattle browse,
After the crops produced by ploughs
Are safely stack'd or put in mows;
Or beans and peas, laid out in rows,
That love refreshing showers and dews,
Are sold by him Pandora knows.——

This is the man whose genial throes—
For human weal—and mankind's woes,
Constrains—the secret to disclose,—

I'LL VOTE FOR JOCE.

WILSON, PRINTER, BOOKBINDER AND ENGRAVER, BRIDGE STREET, BIDEFORD.

Left: *Election leaflets are extremely rare survivals – most people throw them away – but, as this spoof specimen from 1855 shows, humorous ones were more likely to be kept.* (PC)

Right: *Thought to be an election meeting sometime in the 1920s when the electorate were perhaps more interested than today, this picture was taken behind the Pannier Market looking down from Victoria Terrace – and not a bare head to be seen.* (PC)

Above: *A civic occasion in the old cattle market in Honestone Street, c.1900. In 2004 it houses various industrial units and is greatly changed, but the houses in the background are still standing.* (PC)

Right: *A fine study of Wickham's shop in High Street on an unidentified occasion, c.1900. Note the policeman in his military-looking helmet and the crowd of curious boys.* (BL)

the good of the town and its inhabitants. Initially, rate collections were made from door-to-door by the serjeants-at-mace or the police. Sadly, in 1846, the then policeman/collector ran off with a large sum of money after a disagreement over his wages! As with all public bodies economies have been a constant refrain, although in 1887 the council managed to reschedule its debts and thus free up £10,000, which it used for various improvements. Income, apart from the rates, has always been low, but it increased in 1949 following the first imposition of car-parking charges in the town 'to help the ratepayers'. Occasionally the council has sold property and in 1958 it earned £7,500 from the sale of the cattle market in Honestone Street. Even more occasionally the council has been given money, as in the early 1900s when Andrew Carnegie gave £2,200 towards the erection of the still-existing library, and in 2003 when the Bridge Trust gave money towards the Queen's jubilee fountain on the Quay.

The various schemes the council has undertaken cover a wide range and many have already been detailed in other chapters. However, in 1836 the town was first lit with gas and the first policeman employed. Eleven years later there were riots over high food prices and the council purchased a large quantity of flour to sell to the poor cheaply and defuse the situation. In 1850 the foundation-stone of the new Town Hall was laid, whilst six years later the *Bideford Gazette* began trading and the proceedings of the councillors were given the not-always-welcome light of publicity.

A year later (1857) a public subscription led by the Mayor raised the then-large sum of £300 to defray the cost of widening the riverbank along what is Victoria

Park in 2004 and to provide a very pleasant walkway. In 1859 the Bideford Volunteer Rifle Corps was formed with the full backing of the Mayor and council. Over the next decade the council sanctioned the construction of eight almshouses in Meddon Street by James Haycroft, an expatriate Bidefordian (1868), and the provision of Public Rooms in Bridgeland Street (1869). The Meddon Street hospital (1873) and the first public library and art school in what is at the time of writing the Freemasons' Lodge in Bridgeland Street (1875) soon followed. In 1881 the council purchased the manorial rights from John Clevland of Tapeley Park and thus gained control of the Pannier Market and the Quay. Two years later they rebuilt the Market Hall – with the temporarily displaced market being held in Meddon Street.

Amongst all these important events the usual small concerns of local politics were always bubbling under the surface. Thus, when in 1886 the council voted to remove the posts set into the roadway in front of the Strand, a furore ensued. These posts were associated with the old ropemaking industry and became a real cause célebre in the town – so much so that a contemporary writer recounting 'The Battle of the Posts' believed that they influenced a council election 'to such an extent that three of the old members (supporters of the council's policy) were badly beaten at the poll, and had to give way to three new men.'

Two years later the council were constructing a new borough cemetery along with a much-needed reservoir, although the largest new development came in 1889 when the Quay was widened. This was carried out 'notwithstanding differences of opinion as to certain proposed alterations in the

Above: *The Strand with the ropemaking posts present. The buildings remain but the posts have gone.* (PC)

Left: *In 1886 Bideford lost its status as a port. After a long battle this was restored in August 1928 and, to mark the occasion, the local MP Sir Basil Peto and his wife presented this magnificent silver model of a ship to the town. It is now in the Mayor's Parlour in the Town Hall.* (PC)

concluding portions of the task.' Rather oddly the new Quay wall was built 2 feet 6 inches higher than ordered, but the council still had to pay for it. This dispute raged through 1890 but the councillors found time to purchase 'Major Hogg's marshes' which they envisaged as 'a People's Park' in the future. Before this could happen the Pill had to be filled in and preliminary work began in 1896, being completed two years later. The park was eventually opened, as Victoria Park, in 1912.

To herald the new century, construction was initiated in 1904 on the new Municipal Buildings and they were opened along with the library in 1906 – the same year as the Kingsley statue was unveiled. The library was to become home to the town's first museum two years later when Inkerman Rogers organised and labelled a very mixed collection of artefacts and curios.

An interesting reflection on changing lifestyles came in 1910 when the councillors passed a motion expressing strong concern at the damage being done to the town's roads from the increasing numbers of motor vehicles. World events overtook these worries, however, and during the First World War the council did its bit to support both those who joined the Forces and those who worked on the war effort at home. The end of hostilities saw the council buying Chudleigh Fort to use as the site of a war memorial. On a more practical note the council planned to mark peace with a swimming-pool (though it was never built) and gave a dinner in the Pannier Market to 900 local demobilised men.

The post-war depression saw high unemployment and the arrival in the Torridge of some 23 redundant ships. The shortage of jobs was seriously exacerbated by the closure of the collar factory in the Strand and, in 1924, the closure of Hansen's shipyard after it had constructed eight steel ships. On top of all these worries the Old Town Boys' School burnt down in 1926 with damage being put at £4,000.

After such a long spell of bad news councillors doubtless welcomed the occupation of the town's first purpose-built council-houses at Handy Cross in 1926 – at a rent of 8s. per week. The following year Kingsley Road was opened, thus avoiding the narrow bottleneck of North Road, and the council took delivery of its first motorised fire-engine which they named Grenville. Bideford's strong American links were acknowledged in 1929 when the Mayor of Biddeford, Maine visited the town and opened a new 'parking ground' near the Kingsley statue.

During the interwar years Bideford was growing rapidly and in 1936 the Mayors of Bideford and Barnstaple met to discuss a Regional Planning Scheme for future developments along the Taw–Torridge estuary. Sadly, this hopeful future was overshadowed by the first Air Raid Precaution training scheme being set up by the council following government legislation. The war years saw many changes in the town, as detailed in Chapter 11.

The 'austerity years' following the war saw the council severely hampered in what it could do and it was not until 1950 that the first post-war improvements were made, when electric lights replaced the old gas lamps in the streets. Two years later the first female Mayor, Mrs M. Cox, a noted author, was elected, and the following year the first woman sat on the Manor Court jury. Striking a very modern note the

Above: *The frontage of the town hospital in Meddon Street, c.1920. It later became a maternity unit and is a retirement home in 2004.* (PC)

Left: *The Town Council, resplendent in bowlers and top hats, parade past the hospital which had been built in Meddon Street in 1887. The event was probably one of the annual 'Hospital Days' which raised money for the locally-run service.*

Below left: *Another Town Council parade in Meddon Street by the hospital. Note the monkey-puzzle trees in every garden. The railings disappeared in the scrap metal drives of the Second World War.* (PC)

Below: *Inside the spartan-looking Meddon Street hospital in the interwar years.* (PC)

This rather faded photograph shows Market Hill before the Bridge Antiques building replaced the sweet shop on the corner. (BL)

The Borough Fire Brigade wearing their ceremonial uniforms, c.1900. Left to right, back row: Lloyd, Champion, ?, Shortridge, Glover, Chief Officer Chowins; front row: Lee, ?, Hearn, Babb.

The Mayor leading celebrations for the silver jubilee of George V in 1935. (PC)

The Town Council processing up Clovelly Road in May 1907 to attend the Devon County Show which was being held in Bideford that year. The Mayor is preceded by the town crier. (SO)

council were discussing the purchase of land in Kingsley Road in 1955 for use as a 'Helicopter Drome'.

On a more prosaic level, the first 'slum clearances' began in 1957 with the demolition of unfit properties in Hart Street, Vinegar Hill and Bull Hill. Demolition later included New Street, Prospect and Pimlico Places and this was followed by new building with the Copps Close sheltered-housing scheme opening in 1965 at a cost of £75,000. Four years later the old Palace Cinema in Bridgeland Street became the West Country's largest supermarket and in 1972 the council began planning, but luckily never built, a five-storey car park in Bridge Street. In 1973 St Mary's Infant School was constructed in Chanter's Road to replace the Church Infants' School, which by then was showing its age.

In 1974 the single largest change in the Town Council's history occurred when Torridge District Council was set up and took over all the council's property. This severely curtailed the town's ability to run itself as only nine of Torridge's 36 councillors were from Bideford seats. The Town Council has, however, continued to take a major role in the town's affairs, even to the extent of taking back the running of the Pannier Market in 1991 and undertaking an ambitious refurbishment scheme which has left the building looking better than it did for many years.

In the early-twenty-first century the council were active participants in the debate over the new Quay, as well as commissioning the 24-nozzle fountain on the Quay. Enlarged to 16 members, in 2004 the council still meets in the Town Hall where it sits surrounded by portraits of past Mayors – a living link with Bideford's past but yet a body dedicated to the prosperous future of the town.

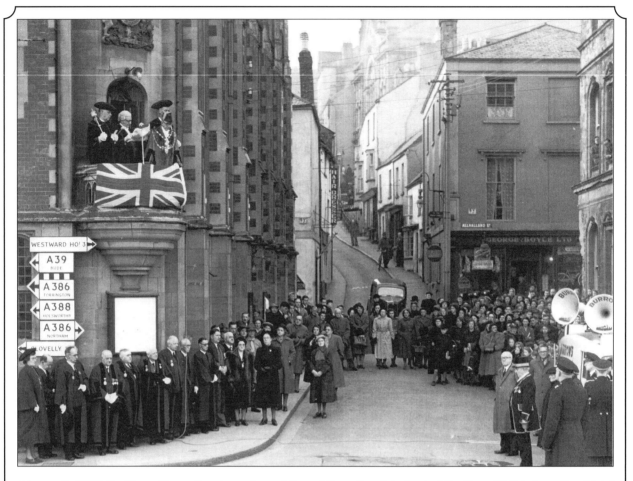

Above: In 1952 the Town Council and members of the public gathered in front of the Town Hall to hear the official announcement of the accession of Queen Elizabeth II following the death of her father, George VI. (HC)

The Mayor, E. Tattersill, unveils the Kingsley statue which was erected to honour the writer who virtually created the town's tourist industry with his book Westward Ho!. (LM)

A long-lost view in which the Kenwith stream, that flows under the Pill in 2004, is redirected prior to its culverting, c.1890. (BL)

Above: *The council worked hard to maintain a water-supply for the town. Jennet's reservoir, here seen frozen over in February 1947, was part of that system.* (HC)

Above: *Victoria Park was opened in 1912 and an early feature of it, now long gone, was the ornamental shelter and clock tower shown in this photograph. The flagpole, which still exists at the time of writing, came from an old ship which was used as an isolation hospital in the estuary.* (LM)

Below: *The site of Hogg's Corner at the end of the bridge just prior to its demolition and the extension of the Town Hall, seen just to the right.* (AB)

Left: *The mayor, Mrs E.M. Cox, meeting the Duke of Edinburgh when he came to open the newly-enlarged Victoria Park in 1952.* (PC)

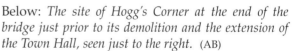

The arrival of the Grenville fire-engine in Bideford saw the council present for the naming ceremony. (PC)

J **HOUSING COMMITTEE.**
22nd November, 1945.

Present : Councillor W. H. Chubb (Mayor), Councillor F. T. Upton (Chairman), Aldermen Huxham and Burton and Councillors Bright, Lang, Chope and Short.

(90) The Minutes of the previous meeting were confirmed.

(91) HOUSING RENT ARREARS.—The Assistant Accountant reported on the rent arrears in respect of both Housing Estates.
Instructions were given to press for payment in a number of cases.

(92) TEMPORARY HOUSING.—(a) General : The Borough Surveyor reported that steady progress is being made in the preparation of the sites at the Grenville Estate : 19 foundations are now ready to receive the bungalows.
(b) Electricity Supplies : A letter was received from the County Council enclosing copy of a letter addressed to the Electricity Supply Company regarding the siting of poles to carry the supplies to the Estate.
The Committee recommend that the County Council's request for an undertaking that the Council will replace the wooden pole sited between " Strathmore " and the Bowden Green Cottages by a steel one when obtainable, be agreed to.
(c) Suggested amendment of sites : The Borough Surveyor reported that a Surveyor of the Ministry of Works had suggested that the width of the main estate road be made use of by halving the width of the proposed footpath in favour of the adjacent bungalow sites.
The Committee recommend that this suggestion be not adopted.
(d) Numbering of houses : The Committee recommend that this matter be left to the Chairman and Councillor Short in consultation with the Rating Officer.

(93) PERMANENT HOUSING.—(a) Barton Field Site : The Borough Surveyor reported that the layout plan of this site had been approved by the Ministry of Health subject to minor amendments.
The working drawings, specifications and bills of quantities were receiving attention.
With regard to the acquisition of this site, a letter was received from the District Valuer stating that he hoped to be in a position to forward his completed negotiation report shortly. The Town Clerk was authorised to defer action to proceed under Compulsory Powers Order pending receipt of the District Valuer's final report.
The Committee recommend that provision be made in the layout of this site for footpath access into Pollyfield Playing Fields.
(b) Avon Road Site : The Town Clerk reported that he had heard nothing further from the owners in respect of the proposed purchase of this land by the Council.

(94) COMMUNAL INSTITUTE, EAST-THE-WATER.—The Committee recommend that the Town Clerk make enquiries as to the possibility of obtaining assistance by means of a grant or otherwise, for the provision of a Communal Institute in the neighbourhood of Sentry Coner, in connection with the Barton Field Housing Site and that the Borough Surveyor report on the availability of a site and the possibility of amending the layout accordingly.

Left: The council's minutes from November 1945 record the inception of the Barton Field estate at East-the-Water. (BTC)

Below: The first of 50 planned prefabricated houses being opened on the Grenville estate in April 1946. The opening ceremony was carried out by the Mayor, Councillor W.H. Chubb. The estate still exists but long ago brick-built houses replaced the utilitarian but much-loved prefabs. (NDJ)

Above and right: *In the 1960s a large number of old houses in Bideford were demolished, being unfit for habitation. They included these houses in New Street and Pimlico Place.* (MS & AB)

Below: *The top of the High Street was once the site of these houses which were long ago demolished by the council to speed the flow of traffic.* (HC)

Above: *The Town Council wear their new ceremonial robes for the first time as they attend church on Manor Court Sunday in April 1951.* (PC)

Below: *This magnificent piece of silver was presented to* HMS Bideford *by the Town Council in December 1931. The then Mayor, Thomas Burton, and his Mayoress are seen with the plate prior to its presentation. It was later returned to the town when the ship was decommissioned and resides in the Mayor's Parlour in 2004.* (PC)

This building was known as the Manor House and stood on the Quay just in front of where the Post Office is at the time of writing. (PC)

Above: *The promenade on the quay provided by the council, along with its bandstand.* (PC)

Chapter 11

Danger, Losse and Detriment

Bideford's charter of 1610 gave the Justices of the Peace or magistrates power to enquire into 'all manner of murthers, felonies, poisonings, inchantments, witchcrafts [and] sorceries...' Problems like these, together with wars and civil strife, frequently kept the authorities busy over the next 300 years. Bideford was not such a quiet backwater as might be imagined.

Like other sea ports in the west, Bideford took the Parliamentary side in the Civil War of 1642–46, and Chudleigh Fort was built at a commanding height at East-the-Water. This survives to the time of writing, although the original earthwork has been obliterated by a brick-and-cement reconstruction. Another fort may have been sited at Bull Hill. Bideford men fought in other parts of Devon, and in the battle of Modbury of 1643, an attempt to divert the Royalists from the siege of Plymouth, 'the Bastable and Biddeford men were the first that came on,' driving the enemy from their position and capturing prisoners and weapons. In September 1643, however, Barnstaple and Bideford troops (reported to be 1,500 strong) were badly beaten when trying to capture Torrington and their retreat led directly 'to the very workes of Biddeford'. The next day the town surrendered and, as a Royalist later wrote, 'their spirit of rebellion was reduced, and they remained perfectly neutral to the dreadful end of that unhappy war.'

Not all Bideford men took the Parliamentary side. In 1663 a 'humble petition' was submitted to Charles II, on behalf of Simon Jeffrey, a local sailor, 'haveing for divers years faythfully served his Majesty's own royall Father of ever blessed memory.' Jeffrey had been wounded and imprisoned and was 'so decreeped [decrepit] in all his body' that he was unfit for work. He was awarded a pension of £3 a year. Another Royalist was the lord of the manor, Sir Bevil Grenville, 'a man of great integrity [and] courage', who was killed at the battle of Lansdowne in 1643. His brother, Sir Richard (not the famous Sir Richard who died in the *Revenge*), began the war as a Royalist, changed to Parliament's side in 1643, then rejoined the king a year later, incurring universal distrust and hatred. Nicknamed 'Skellum' (traitor or rascal) Grenville, he died in exile during the Commonwealth.

The Civil War was followed by plague in 1646. Said to have been brought to Bideford in bales of wool from Spain, it spread quickly through the town and, if John Watkins, Bideford's eighteenth-century historian is to be believed, 'In a few weeks, the houses were filled with horror, and the streets covered with grass.'

The parish registers record 229 burials between June and December 1646, most of them presumably plague victims. John Strange, merchant and former Mayor, remained behind when other leading townsmen fled, to try to organise measures to counter the plague. He died the same year, probably himself a victim of the pestilence. His will established a row of almshouses in Meddon Street for the elderly of the town. These, although rebuilt around 1870 and again recently, still fulfil their founder's wishes at the time of writing.

In 1682 the infamous episode of the Bideford witches provided a sensation for the 'foolish rabble'. Popular belief in witchcraft was then very strong, and elderly spinsters or widows with no friends were often blamed for any mysterious aches, pains or fits their neighbours had. When Grace Thomas of Bideford began to suffer in these ways she and her family accused Temperance Lloyd, an old widow. Temperance, who perhaps was a little simple herself, was forced to admit that she had often met the Devil in the shape of a black man, 'in a street called Higher Gunstone Lane', and that she had pinched and pricked Grace. There was a lot more 'evidence' against her, much of which she admitted, so she was soon arrested and locked up. At least she denied having made a model of Grace to stick pins in, but by this time much of Bideford had witch mania and denounced another old lady, Mary Trembles, for making another woman ill. Her companion, Susanna Edwards, was arrested at the same time, also for witchcraft. Some much-exaggerated charges were made and the two women were sent to Exeter to be tried with Temperance Lloyd, who was thought to be the leader of a coven. There was no

Charles I (C. Harding) and his Queen Henrietta Maria (Mrs G. Babb) along with their four children (Mary Harding, Mary Phillips, Doreen and Gwen Babb), a lady-in-waiting (Mrs R. Cock) and Cavalier messenger (R. Cock) in another shot from the 1925 Pageant. (RLK)

These cottages at Old Town, opposite the fire station at the time of writing, were reputed to have been the witches' homes. (PC)

Right: The scene of Temperance Lloyd's alleged meeting with the devil. When this photograph of Gunstone was taken over 200 years later all the houses were white-washed. (PC)

shortage of 'witnesses' coming forward to accuse the three, so they were found guilty. One of the judges, Francis, Lord North, privately found the evidence 'trifling', but fearing the fervour of the people, decided it was safer to sentence the women. They, somewhat unaccountably, were infected by the hysteria and confessed to most of the charges. Mary Trembles was the most 'obstinate' but this did not help her, and Temperance Lloyd continued to assert that she had met the Devil. All were hanged, some of the last witches in England to be so punished. Further rumours of witchcraft were heard from time to time and Martha Lee, the last of a line of reputed witches, died in Bideford Workhouse in 1853 at the age of 105. An even later case occurred in 1901 when Sarah Sayers of Silver Street was gaoled for a month with hard labour after preparing magic charms for an undercover policeman.

Three years after the witch trial, in June 1685, the Duke of Monmouth, the illegitimate son of Charles II, landed at Lyme Regis and rallied an army of disaffected West Country men. At the infamous 'Bloody Assizes' which followed the battle of Sedgemoor, Judge Jeffreys sentenced many rebels to death or transportation. Although no local men are listed among known rebels, some may have taken part, for Bideford was among the towns ordered to display, as a warning to others, a gruesome 'quarter' of a hanged rebel, boiled in pitch.

Bideford burial registers show peaks in the death rate, notably in 1689, 1719, 1733, 1742 and 1755. In 1719 'the small-pox was very mortal in Bideford – inoculation, that blessed preservative of beauty health and life not then being in use.' In 1733 'Epidemick Colds' killed large numbers nationally, and 1742 was marked by another smallpox epidemic. Later, however, there were fewer bad years, possibly because the Bridge Trustees paid for the poor to be inoculated. We have found little information about medical care but that it was fairly rough and ready is shown by a note from 1731 that:

Mr Cheselden took from the Body of Mr Hartwel Buck, eldest son of George Buck of Biddiford in Devonshire Esq: a large stone of 7 Inches and a half round, weighing five ounces and a half In the Space of a Minute.

High burial numbers for the years 1760–62 could include some of the many prisoners of war then in the town. The Seven Years War had broken out in 1756 and two years later a newspaper carried the following report:

Last Sunday morning (October 15), the prisoners in the French prison at Bideford (in number 1050) attempted to make their escape; but were discovered, and fired on by the soldiers on duty, one was killed on the spot, and several others were much wounded. They have attempted to escape twice before, but were timely discover'd.

This prison appears to have been a camp at Pillmouth in Landcross. More French prisoners were sent during the Napoleonic War and some, perhaps many, must have died in captivity. As the whereabouts of their cemetery is unknown, bodies discovered now and then in Bideford are popularly believed to be

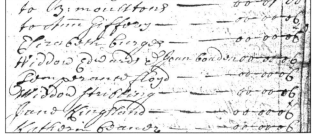

The 'Andrew Dole' book lists the poor who received help from this charity. Note the name Temperance Lloyd from this page dated 1681. A year later this poor old woman was hanged as one of the Bideford 'witches'. Above her name is that of Widdow Edwards – possibly Susanna Edwards, another of the 'witches'.

Weekly Account of Prisoners of War at							the			
Remaining the	Since last Account.						Number now in Custody.	Whereof in		
	Ex.	D.	D.D.	Escaped.	Retaken.	Received from			Prison.	Hospital.
						Ships.	Other Persons.			

This fragment dates from the eighteenth century and was found pasted at the back of a cupboard in a house in Bridgeland Street. It was probably used by the officer in charge of the French PoWs held at Bideford. At the time of writing it is in the Burton Art Gallery and Museum. (BT)

theirs. Skeletons have been found near the gasworks, East-the-Water, which may have been the site of one of the prison camps, and also around Pyne's Lane. However, the 16 skeletons 'laid side by side', discovered on the site of the present library in 1904, indicate an earlier burial-ground, perhaps pre-dating the present churchyard. As recently as July 1985 another body was unearthed in Clovelly Road. Like the others, it consisted solely of bones – flesh, clothing and any coffin having rotted away.

Many Bideford men took part in the wars against Napoleon. Gravestones in Old Town Cemetery record seamen who served at Trafalgar as well as two Waterloo veterans. At the end of the war, large numbers of soldiers and sailors were demobilised, and within a short time an economic depression set in. The Corn Law, which kept the price of bread high, added to the sufferings of the poor. In May 1816 hunger riots took place in Bideford, to prevent a cargo of potatoes being shipped out of the area. The violence was put down by the North Devon Yeomanry, a body of local volunteer cavalry, who arrested four of the ringleaders and took them to Exeter prison. The Home Secretary, Lord Sidmouth, sent a man from London 'to bring to justice the Persons principally concerned in these criminal and dangerous proceedings.' The trial was held in August 1816 and the men were sentenced to terms of imprisonment of between six months and two years. The Yeomanry were later supplemented by the Bideford Rifle Volunteers – a Victorian forerunner of today's Territorial Army.

In 1836 the newly-formed Town Council decided to hire a professional policeman for the first time. It employed Elias Palmer, previously a London 'Peeler', who served the town for 12 years. His job was anything but easy. He survived several murderous attacks from drunken sailors, broke up 'riotous and drunken orgies' in many of the town's pubs, and in 1842 barely escaped 500 people who rioted after he arrested a drunk on the Quay. The police force was enlarged in 1853 to two and later to three men, eventually being merged with the County force in 1889.

The premises in which the town's police force is presently housed dates from 1897. During the nineteenth century the Bideford Association for the Protection of Property, working to discourage criminals and help the police, offered rewards for the capture of thieves.

For prisoners found guilty at their trial, punishments were harsh. In 1843, 13 boys aged between ten and 15 were put in the stocks in rotation to be 'exposed to the public gaze and derision' for throwing stones. In 1828, two thieves were whipped around the town – their arms tied to staves held by parish officials. The staves still exist and are in the council chamber in the Town Hall at the time of writing. If whipping was not enough, vagrants could be sentenced, as John Wray was in 1827, to the treadmill at Exeter Gaol. Transportation was the punishment for crimes considered more serious. In 1736, for example, Matthew Crang was sentenced to seven years for the theft of a few tools worth 5s. George and John Buck often secured the contracts to ship such 'felons' to Virginia and Maryland, where they probably used them as cheap labour on their plantations. A number of convicts from Bideford were sent to Australia in the nineteenth century, mainly thieves found guilty of a second offence. Among them was Jane Willis, who was only 17 when sentenced to ten years for stealing an umbrella in 1841. Joseph Beer, a sheep rustler, got 14 years in 1842.

In 1631 the Corporation recorded that:

... awfull and lamentable experience hath taught us what greate danger, losse and detriment the casualtie of fire hath brought unto this Towne, even unto the utter undoinge of Diverse of the poore Inhabitants.

The fire may have been caused by a spark from a kiln, for potters were thenceforth forbidden to stack furze, which was used in the final stages of firing, near kilns and houses. Town records in 1659 show that a John Hill gave 'Twelve Water Bucketts for the use of the Towne,' and a few years later townspeople were

Bideford men served in the wars of the nineteenth century. William Rogers proudly wears his Crimean medals on the uniform of the Bideford Rifle Volunteers. His son, Inkerman (named after the Crimean War battle) is remembered as a local historian. (AV)

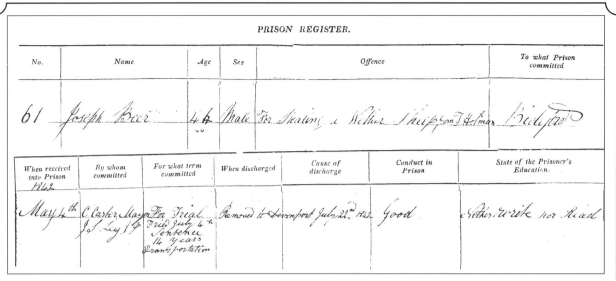

No.	Name	Age	Sex	Offence	To what Prison committed
61	Joseph Beer	46	Male	For Stealing a Wether Sheep from J Helman	Bideford

When received into Prison 1842	By whom committed	For what term committed	When discharged	Cause of discharge	Conduct in Prison	State of the Prisoner's Education.
May 4th	C Carter Mayor J S Ley	For Trial Tried July 6th Sentence 14 years Transportation	Removed to Devonport July 22 1842	Good		Neither Write nor Read

Above: *An extract from the Bideford prison register from 1842 showing that Joseph Beer was transported for 14 years for stealing a sheep.* (NDRO)

Left: *A participant in the 1925 Pageant dressed in the finery of a Napoleonic period officer – a time when Bideford held a prisoner-of-war camp for French sailors and soldiers.* (RLK)

Below: *The mounted band of the North Devon Yeomanry entering Mill Street from North Road, c.1900.* (PC)

The town crier, Jim Weeks, holds two of the old constable's staves in 1985. At one time, offenders had their hands tied to these and, with a constable holding one on each side, were whipped around the town. (PC)

A crowded scene on the iron-parapeted bridge with the North Devon Yeomanry ceremonially parading across. (PC)

ordered to set water-filled barrels at their doors. In 1770 the Bridge Trust gave the town its first fire engine which, with its leather piping, was put 'in a convenient place for its security' – under the Town Hall! It was joined there by a second engine in 1803. Another, the 'West of England' fire-engine, was operated by an insurance company and initially only turned out to fight fires in insured property. A new Exeter-built 'mahogany brigade fire engine constructed on springs', sent by the company in 1847, unfortunately crashed just outside the town. In due course, the fire station was moved to its site at Old Town, but difficulties still occurred. In 1920 the brigade arrived at Edgehill College with a handcart to fight a serious fire. It took 20 minutes to get the water turned on, then one of the mains burst under the unaccustomed pressure. The college was gutted.

Bideford men served abroad in the wars of the nineteenth century but the First World War brought the horrors of modern war to virtually every home in the town. Following the declaration of war against Germany on 4 August 1914 the local Territorial soldiers were immediately called up and 'Every man turned up promptly'. They collected on the Quay where 'a great cheering crowd accompanied them across the Long Bridge to the railway station'. Sadly, it was only weeks later that the first Bidefordian casualty was reported. Captain Thomas Wickham

was a Territorial serving with the Manchester Regiment when he was killed in the first week of September. Voluntary enlistment, later followed by conscription, saw nearly 2,000 local men serving in the forces; of these nearly 200 became casualties. The end of the war in November 1918 saw the men slowly return home. In July 1919 an official 'Peace Day' was held in the town. A massive open-air religious service was staged in Victoria Park along with games and a fancy-dress parade and a dinner for 800–900 demobilised men in the Market Hall.

During the First World War there was no serious risk of enemy action against the town itself, unlike in the Second World War. During the latter no bombs were dropped on the town, but the war created major changes and dislocations to everyday life. In the period leading up to the outbreak of war in September 1939, the Bideford section of the ARP (Air Raid Precautions) began training in earnest. The council ordered 29,000 sandbags and set up a siren on the fire station in Old Town. The absence of air-raid shelters meant that early preparations were primitive in the extreme. Children at the Church school (home to the Angling Club in 2004), for example, were to run over to the Rectory Gardens and hide under the trees whilst

A triumphal arch at the bottom of High Street, possibly around the time of the Boer War when the Yeomanry went off to fight. (PC)

Above: *A section of the Bideford St John Ambulance Brigade parade on the Quay during the Second World War. The uniformed officer at their head is Fred Hockaday and the man in front is Kellow Webb, head teacher of North Bank School.* (HC)

Right: *The Bideford Air-Raid Precautions Rescue Team on a training exercise at Barton Hill, Torquay in October 1943.* (PC)

THE LADS FROM THE TOWN BY THE FORD.

'NEATH the ocean's sheen in the submarine,
 Or skimming the trackless air,
Or watching the foe, with Jellicoe,
 The Bideford lad is there.
Heligoland's Bight, in the Falkland fight,
 In each they have made good record;
They are carving their name on the scroll of fame,
 These lads from the town by the ford.

In the great advance through the plains of France,
 At Mons, Marne, and Charleroi;
Where fighting has been, at the fore they are seen—
 The Bell and the Grammar School Boy.
For the dear white town they are winning renown,
 Her sons have high honors scored;
For Empire and throne they have sailed, steamed, flown,
 The lads from the town by the ford.

At the Suez Canal, at the Dardanelle,
 They are wielding Old England's sword,
At their country's need they replied with speed,
 These lads from the town by the ford.
Leaving Devon's home, they have crossed the foam,
 That victory might be assured;
They will not be beat, they know no defeat,
 These lads from the town by the ford.

We can proudly tell how brave Stucley fell,
 At the head of his Grenadiers;
"On lads," his cry, as he fell to die,
 Finding a soldier's bier.
'Mongst the first to fall at the Empire's call,
 'Neath the blow of the German horde,
Fell a Wickham, true, staunch Ascott too,
 Brave sons of the town by the ford.

Ackland, Luxton and Rose, fell facing our foes,
 To uphold England's plighted word;
Jewell, Kemp, Smalldon fell, there a Wicketts as well,
 Upholding their town by the ford.
She has sent her sons to fight the huns—
 Aye! sent forth many a score,
O'er the dear bridge, cross the brown sand ridge,
 If wanted, she still sends more—
For aye to the front, to bear the brunt,
 To uphold their sires record.
As in days of yore, they are at the fore,
 These lads from the town by the ford.

JAMES C. HARDING, White House Infirmary, Bideford, Devon.

WILSON BROS., PRINTERS, BIDEFORD.

Right: *One of the 1,800 Bideford men, known to us only as 'Charles', who flocked to join the Local Defence Volunteers in May 1940. He wears his LDV armband and carries a rifle with fixed bayonet – his stance and age suggests a First World War veteran.* (NDRO)

Left: *A poignant poem published as a broadsheet during the First World War when many of the 'boys' celebrated by the poet died during the fighting.* (PW)

The 1st Platoon of the Bideford Home Guard in 1941 proudly display some of their weapons in this photograph taken in Victoria Park. (PC)

Below: *A Civil Defence demonstration in the summer of 1939 in Victoria Park. The two 'patients' are Alice Friend and Mary Cleaver. The man fanning them is H. Cleaver, with C. Dipstale in the foreground and A. Grant at the back.* (HC)

Above: *A fine view of some members of the Bideford Auxiliary Fire Service with their portable pumping apparatus.* (HC)

Below: *The Bideford Home Guard soon had its own band, shown here in Victoria Park.* (DF)

those in the infant school in Lower Meddon Street had to make their way to the crypt of St Mary's Church.

Shortly after war was declared a leaflet went to every household in Britain telling people what to do, although this was slightly alarmist. Blackout conditions became normal, air-raid wardens were appointed in most streets, first-aid posts were established in Meddon Street and at East-the-Water, and an emergency mortuary was opened in the chapel at Old Town Cemetery. A total of 11 public shelters were eventually built to supplement premises with suitable basements. Two fire-engines and seven trailer pumps were also on standby together with a fire-fighting launch on the Torridge, in case the town's antiquated mains burst. Bags of sand were hung from lampposts to be used to extinguish the expected incendiary bombs.

In May 1940, following a period known as the 'Phoney War', Prime Minister Neville Chamberlain called for the setting up of the Local Defence Volunteers. At Bideford 1,800 men came forward for the LDV which, reduced to a more manageable size, became the 5th Battalion (Bideford) Devon Home Guard, with its headquarters at 6 The Quay (the Mr Chips restaurant at the time of writing). Its first weapons were rifles borrowed from the cadets of a London school evacuated to Westward Ho!. Later weapons included officially-issued rifles, machine-guns, mortars, rubber truncheons and even pikes. Training was carried out at the Sports Ground, and later on a meadow by Ford Farm. Bideford men built and manned at least seven roadblocks around the town, some made of sandbags and empty oil drums, others of concrete and barbed wire. They considered setting up a 'flame trap' of petrol sprays, near the present Rydon Garage, and actually built a block-house with chains across the road opposite Clifton Terrace, East-the-Water. Invasion scares on the nights of 19/20 June and 7/8 September 1940 brought the whole battalion out to man the defences, but luckily no Nazis came. 'The great difficulty of defending Bideford, both West and East-the-Water, was the high

hills on both sides of the river,' wrote the Home Guard commander later – words surely echoing those of the Civil War generals 300 years before. The Home Guard decided to give priority to defending both ends of the bridge. Further defences were added as the war continued – the Admiralty erected 'dragons' teeth' along the Quay, and two anti-aircraft guns were placed on the roof of the Strand Cinema.

Luckily no German invasion took place, but others did. In June 1940 the first evacuees began to arrive in the town and within six months some 2,198 had arrived and been billeted on the generally welcoming population. The Bideford Women's Emergency Committee swung into action to collect blankets and produce straw-filled mattresses for the newcomers. They also staffed emergency telephones and began knitting gloves, scarves and pullovers for service personnel. Sadly, the council minutes of the period are full of items critical of the London children billeted in the town, and the way they acted towards the locals, but some made friends and even settled in Bideford after the war.

At this date there were few servicemen and women in the town as their services were more urgently required on the South Coast – but units of the Auxiliary Military Pioneer Corps were stationed in the town. Formed from refugees from Czechoslovakia, Germany and Austria they included some famous personalities such as Coco the Clown and Max Jaffa, who put on shows for adults and children alike in the town. Also in 1940, the Rola Works was opened on what is the site of the Esso garage at the time of writing, to produce pumps for aeroplanes. They employed some 600 people and their products were vital to keep the RAF flying.

In 1941 the Bideford Air Training Corps was formed to provide training to youths before they were called up. The Bideford Sea Cadets followed in 1942. Another youth organisation was the Bideford Messenger Corps which consisted of some 61 boys and girls who, 'all with their parents' permission' were to deliver urgent messages to link the

H.V. Cope reviews the Bideford Air-Raid Wardens on the Quay by Bridge Buildings during the war. (HC)

Above: *The Bideford Fire Brigade in the 1920s with many of the men wearing their First World War medals. The photograph was taken in front of Bridge Buildings.* (BL)

Right: *During the great drought of 1976 Bideford Fire Brigade drove to Silford Lake to wash down their engine, such was the shortage of water.* (BB)

A very rare shot of First World War female workers taken at Bartlett's Yard, East-the-Water in 1916. They had taken the place of the men who were away fighting. (PC)

Above: *During the Second World War Bideford Quay was covered in defensive concrete blocks known as 'dragon's teeth'. Here the council steam engine is being used to put the blocks in place.* (BTC)

Left: *The Mayor, J.H. Bright, having cake with a group of local women who helped with the flood of evacuees to Bideford in 1940. The armband on the man to the right reads 'Evacuation Reception Officer.'* (PC)

Right: *Bideford's anti-aircraft guns were mounted on the roof of the Strand Cinema. Wartime vehicles can be seen parked on the Pill below.* (PC)

Above: *A detachment of Home Guard march past the Kingsley statue.* (HC)

Right: *The interior of the Second World War Rola factory in Kingsley Road which produced secret equipment for the RAF.* (HC)

Left: *Servicemen preparing PLUTO (Pipeline Under The Ocean) for trial at Bank End, Bideford, probably in 1944.* (NDMT)

Above: *Ceremonial parades were common as morale-boosters during the war and here is one of them – with representatives from all three services.* (HC)

Left: *A wartime parade along the Quay in Bideford headed by the Town Marshal.* (PC)

emergency services, the council officials and the Home Guard. Each supplied their own bicycles and wore 'distinctive armlets'.

In August 1941 the Bideford Invasion Committee was set up to plan for the unthinkable. Most of its time was spent planning how such buildings as Geneva School and Edgehill College could become 'Shadow Hospitals' (for emergency usage). Meanwhile, the whole town became involved in salvage drives and 'Digging for Victory'. A specimen allotment was laid out in Victoria Park to show would-be gardeners how to grow food efficiently. A civic restaurant, to supply cheap but nutritious meals, was set up in the Church Lads' Brigade Hall in Allhalland Street, and a little later another one was opened in the Pannier Market. To allow more women to help the war effort a nursery was opened in Bridge Street by Mrs O. Jenn with a second being opened in 1942 in the BAAC premises on the Pill. Postwomen were seen for the first time in the town and women used the Bowling Club as a collection point for fruit used to produce jam.

The ornamental railings and gates seen in so many old photographs of the town were targeted in scrap drives, with collection beginning in May 1943. Much of this material was carried away by a host of small coastal craft, which were using Bideford port and making it busier than it had been for many years.

By 1942 the Americans had joined the war and large numbers of US service personnel began to arrive in the town. They proved very popular and made many lasting friendships. The American Red Cross opened a club for them at 'Upover' in East-the-Water and at Christmas 1943 some 900 local children were treated by American soldiers to films and sweets at the Strand Cinema. Many of the officers lived with Bideford families, who much appreciated the food they brought with them in those days of rationing. Some friendships blossomed into romance, and a number of marriages were celebrated before the GIs went off to the Normandy landings in 1944. A tree with a plaque commemorating their stay was planted in Victoria Park in 1945 and still survives at the time of writing.

As the war situation improved, so the Home Guard became less vital, and on the last day of 1944 the local unit was stood down and, five months later, the end of war in Europe was greeted with 'wild jubilation'. The Prime Minister's announcement was broadcast from loudspeakers on the Quay and dances erupted all over the town, the one in Meddon Street going on 'by the light of searchlights till the early hours of the morning.'

Although years of 'austerity' had to be faced after the war, and Bideford has not escaped social ills such as unemployment, recent times have seen one of the less eventful periods in the town's history. Tribulations, like the collapse of a bridge arch in 1968, and a drought in 1976, which put the town on 'standpipes', look insignificant compared with the violence, epidemics and harsh justice endured by the people of the past.

Right: *On 1 May 1941 a part-time nursery was set up in the Sunday schoolroom of the Bridge Street Methodist Church and continued to run until March 1950. It provided care for the children of both evacuees and working mothers. The adults in this photograph are Mrs Olive Jenn, Miss Blackwell and Mrs Holroyd.* (JJ)

BOROUGH OF BIDEFORD
AND BIDEFORD RURAL DISTRICT

ALFRED E. BLACKWELL
CHIEF BILLETING OFFICER

Telephone:
BIDEFORD 267.

EVACUATION OFFICE,
BRIDGE BUILDINGS,
BIDEFORD, DEVON.

14th January, 1946.

Dear Mr. Lee,

On relinquishing the position of Chief Billeting Officer I should like to express to you and your Staff my warm appreciation of the help and many kindnesses which have been extended to me and to the cause of the Government Evacuation Scheme in this district.

It has been a difficult time for many of us but as far as this department is concerned the arduous tasks have been rendered lighter and more pleasant by the excellent relations which have existed between our respective offices and the spirit of co-operation which has prevailed.

Mrs. Golding, who has been a valued assistant during the latter years, succeeds me, to deal with the remaining Evacuation problems.

I am,

Yours very sincerely,

Montague F. Lee, Esq.,
"Bideford Gazette" Office,
Grenville Street,
Bideford.

Above: *As wartime evacuees arrived in Bideford so they were met and fed by volunteers, as in this picture taken at the Bethel Rest Room in East-the-Water.* (PC)

Above: *A letter of thanks from the Chief Evacuation Officer Alfred Blackwell to Monty Lee, editor of the Bideford Gazette.* (HC)

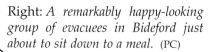

Right: *A remarkably happy-looking group of evacuees in Bideford just about to sit down to a meal.* (PC)

Above: *Local groups of servicemen and women on parade on the Quay some time during the Second World War.* (PC)

Right: *US troops were stationed in the Bideford area in large numbers prior to D-Day, and here we see a ceremonial march past on the Quay.* (HC)

Below: *Young evacuees sleeping on pallet beds at their temporary accommodation in Bideford in 1941.* (PC)

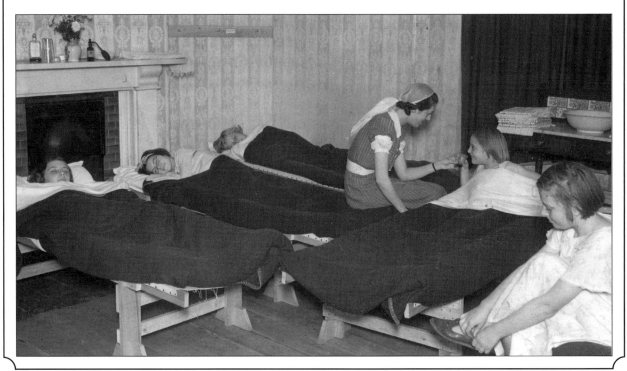

Above: *Rationing hit everyone hard. In December 1945 Wickham's wine merchants in High Street obtained a supply of Australian sherry and this queue resulted – even though shoppers were limited to just one bottle each.* (BP)

Right: *This photograph was taken during the test launching of an assault craft from a road transporter, to determine the best way to cross the Rhine.* (NDMT)

Left: *In the first years of the 1950s the Korean War broke out and the British Army were involved. Amongst the prisoners captured by the Communist North Koreans was Monty Cawsey of Bideford who was held for 18 months. Here we see him being met at Bideford railway station where a crowd several hundred strong cheered him as he arrived.* (NDJ)

Above: *On VE Day, 1945, there were joyrides aboard landing-craft and naval boats on the Torridge.* (HC)

BIDEFORD BOROUGH " CIVIL DEFENCE RESCUE PARTIES ".

RESCUE TRAINING PROGRAMME. Week commencing September
=========================== 27th, 1943.

Air Raid Precaution Officer
    and Borough Organiser;- T. Burton, Esqr
County Approved;-
    "Rescue Training Instructors;- F.R.Gray,
    "   "   " A.F.Beer,
                                   E.W.Cox,

Forewword;- The duty of a Rescue Party is as follows;-

(a) To rescue living persons trapped in wreckage.
(b) To recover the bodies of persons, where this can be
    done without further risk of life.
(c) To salvage essential food stocks provided the Party
    is not deflected from saving life.
(d) To render such first-aid that lie within their power.

Normally, Rescue Parties are not called upon to undertake
    substantial demolition or shoring during Rescue
    operations, unless such works are necessary to save
    life, or to safeguard life.

PROGRAMME;-

(I).   (a) Wanstead method of blanketting a stretcher.

            (b) Use of 40 foot 1½" lashing on a stretcher
                illustrating method of slinging Stretchers
                by the use of :- (I) Bowline on a bight knot
                                  (2) Double sheet bend.

            (c) Using King Stretcher harness.

            (d) Method of using "Trigg Lift" ;- (a) Speed lift.
                                                 (b) Ordinary Lift.
                                                 (c) Heavy Lift.
            Questions.

(2),-   (a) Using Remote Breathing Apparatus.
                Explanation and reasons of its necessity.

            (b) Sizes and strengths of ropes;- Scaffold hitch.
                                                Chair knot.

            (c) Markings on Casualties.

(3),-   (a) Use of Machinery to multiple effect,-

            (a) Straight Lever.

            (b) Folding Wedge.

            (c) Wedge;- Screw Jack.
                         Rachet Jack.
                         Hydraulic Jack.

            (d) Wheel on pulleys;- Single and Snatch block.
                                    Double Block.
                                    Treble Block.

            (e) Reeving tackle.

Luckily Bideford was never attacked during the war, but the Civil Defence workers trained hard to prepare for any eventuality. This page from a typical training programme shows some of the skills they had to learn. (HC)

Chapter 12

Matters Spiritual

The religious history of any town mirrors national events to some extent, but nonconformity, which 'took root very early', played a more important part in Bideford than most places.

In the sixteenth century, Bideford appears to have accepted the overthrow of the Church of Rome by Henry VIII and Edward VI, taking no part in the Catholic 'Prayer Book Rebellion' of 1549, which affected Exeter and other parts of the county. In Elizabeth I's reign, the long struggle with Spain produced a strong reaction against Roman Catholicism, especially among seamen, who risked the Inquisition if captured. Meanwhile, an interest in strict Protestantism was aroused by trading contacts with strongly Calvinist places such as La Rochelle.

In 1641, the puritan William Bartlett was appointed 'Lecturer' in St Mary's, as part of a Parliamentary policy to counteract Royalist clergy. The Independent Congregation was set up in 1648, and Bartlett added

insult to injury by using material from the rectory to repair his own house. The vicar, Arthur Giffard, was forcibly ejected by cavalry. According to his supporters, they 'used him barbarously making him all over dirt, and some spitting at him as he passed along the street.' A later writer also noted that:

The pious, or rather impious reformers threw the baptismal font out of the church as a relique of the Whore of Babylon's abominations; and one schismatic, to shew his zeal the more conspicuously, appropriated it to the purpose of a trough for his swine to feed out of; and if he had his deserts, he would have made one of their company.

After the Restoration Bartlett was 'dismist' in his turn, accused of using 'reviling language against the Royall family', although another account says he merely refused to subscribe to the Act of Uniformity

The magnificent memorial to Sir Thomas Granfyld in St Mary's Church – one of the few ancient memorials to survive the Victorian rebuilding of the 1860s. (PS)

The Norman font photographed when it stood in front of the tower doors and screen. It is inset with fine carvings from the medieval period. (PC)

Above: *A print of St Mary's Church prior to rebuilding. There appear to be two sets of gates – both to the churchyard and Church Walk.* (PC)

Left: *An undated church service at St Mary's sometime before the First World War. Members of the Boys' Brigade band are in the forefront with the resplendent town crier behind.* (PC)

Below: *The Silver Street Wesleyan/Bible Christian Sunday School gather with their three teachers in this photograph from 1913.* (JC)

The twin spires of Lavington United Reform Church are a Bideford landmark. Nicholas Pevsner described them as 'spiky Gothic'. (PC)

of 1662. He and his son John continued to preach in secret in and around Bideford for another 20 years, despite fines and imprisonment.

In June 1670, for example, five Bideford constables surprised a prayer meeting in the house of Mistress Sarah Dennis being taken by John Bartlett. Both he and Sarah were fined £20, whilst the rest of the congregation were fined 5s. each. Another raid in 1671 found 40 people present. A religious census of 1678 shows that Bideford had 2,500 churchgoers and just 96 nonconformists.

After the Toleration Act of 1689, the Bartletts' successors, John Bowden and James Wood, could legally hold services, but reports that Wood had had an affair with an Irish girl caused the congregation to split. In 1694 his supporters established the 'Little Meeting' in a building in the High Street (behind what is Clinton Cards at the time of writing), while the rest, under Bowden, formed the 'Great Meeting' in 1696 on the site still occupied by Lavington Chapel. Daniel Defoe wrote in the early-eighteenth century:

Here is a very large well-built and well finish'd meeting-house, and by the multitude of people which I saw come out of it, and the appearance of them, I thought all the town had gone thither.

Seven years after the arrival in 1753 of Samuel Lavington, whose 'amiable disposition made every person his friend', the two congregations were re-united. In 1787 Lavington and the rector set up the first Sunday schools, which were jointly funded – an early example of ecumenism. Lavington's ministry lasted for 57 years and, in 1869, the new chapel in Bridgeland Street was named in his honour. It was extended in 1923 and still serves the town in the early-twenty-first century.

Another group of local nonconformists were the refugee French Protestants or Huguenots. Among the earliest was the Sieur de St Michel, whose daughter Elisabeth married Samuel Pepys. The site of Bideford's French church, established by 1694, is unknown, but in the 1730s its octogenarian minister, M. Roman, was serving Barnstaple as well. The Huguenots, never numerous, were eventually assimilated into English congregations.

Divisions among Bideford's nonconformists in the seventeenth and eighteenth centuries appear insignificant compared with happenings at St Mary's. Nicholas Eaton, who succeeded Giffard as rector, had been earlier dismissed as first President of Harvard College in New England, for 'inhumanity to the students'. A nonconformist writer alleged that he became a 'bitter persecutor of nonconformists', and died in a debtors' prison. His successor, Michael Ogilby, appointed in 1674, was mainly noted for rebuilding the parsonage and battling with his congregation. In 1680 he was presented to the local Quarter Sessions for drunkenness, abusing a churchgoer 'to the great greife of the people then and there assembled,' using 'unchristian-like language' to the town clerk, and telling the Bishop's messenger that 'he could find it in his heart to kill him.' In spite of all this, Ogilby remained Bideford's vicar until his death in 1699.

A peaceful interlude followed, when the chief excitements were the installation of an organ in 1728 plus a new 'Great Roof' for the church in 1733. A graveyard was opened at the top of Honestone Street in 1742, a year of high mortality. Then John Whitfield was instituted, and 'for nearly forty years the civil and ecclesiastical government of Bideford exhibited a constant state of warfare.' In an open letter to Whitfield, Lewis Buck, a vicar of Abbotsham, and one of Whitfield's chief adversaries, accused him of abusing the congregation from the pulpit, calling them 'Rogues, Scoundrells, Villains, Smugglers, Scum of the Earth, [and] People worse than ye Inhabitants of Sodom and Gomorrah.' The letter continued:

People are almost all afraid to go to the Church. Pray Sir, how many may you have spit in the face of in the Church! How many have you collar'd and even struck in the Church?

In 1750 Whitfield broke open the town record room under the vestry floor, lugging the deeds and

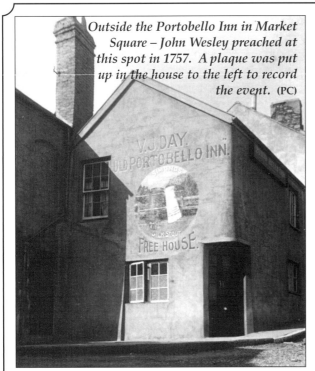

Outside the Portobello Inn in Market Square – John Wesley preached at this spot in 1757. A plaque was put up in the house to the left to record the event. (PC)

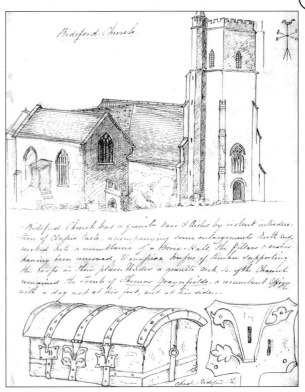

Above: *A drawing from the Harding Manuscripts in the North Devon Athenaeum showing Bideford Church prior to its rebuildings which left only the tower as an original feature.* (NDA)

Left: *The front page of the Bideford Wesleyan magazine from 1907 showing a variety of advertisers supporting the cause.* (PC)

Right: *Huguenot congregations received money from the Royal Bounty, for their poor members. This distribution list of 1729 was signed by Monsieur Roman, the pastor, and Abraham Cosseratt, a rich Huguenot merchant, one of the elders. Elizabeth Seugnet, Madeleine Touzein and Marie La Palme received 16s.5d. each.*

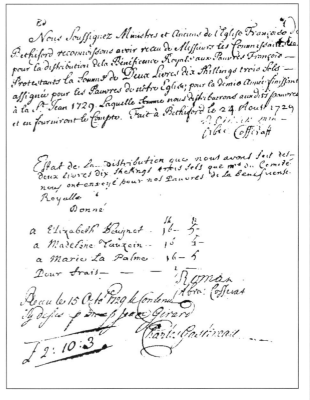

Left: *This panoramic view shows the scholars of the Bideford Wesleyan Sunday School crossing the bridge on their way to Instow for their annual treat, c.1908. They are led by the chapel band.* (PC)

Above: *Bridge Street Methodist Chapel shortly before its demolition – what a superb public hall this would have made for Bideford!* (AB)

Left: *Another shot of the 'Nonconformist Cathedral of North Devon', otherwise known as the Methodist chapel in Bridge Street. Since demolished, its role has been taken over by the building in High Street.* (PS)

Below: *An advertising postcard from c.1910 showing the organ in the High Street Methodist chapel.* (LM)

papers to the Town Hall and hurling them at the astonished Mayor and magistrates. At the same time he left a coffin with the body of a three-year-old child on the floor of the same room, refusing to bury it. The quarrel was finally taken to the Court of King's Bench but, although Whitfield had to bury the child, the townspeople were denied the use of the vestry room for parish meetings. Thenceforward they met in the new Bridge Hall, summoned by a bell, which is in the Burton Art Gallery and Museum at the time of writing and which carried the inscription: 'Our parson's pride form'd me a bell, By that I rose that satan fell.'

Whitfield's prayer, 'Pray God deliver me from this Place and this People,' was not answered until 1783, for he was 'unhappily for the welfare of the parish, spared to a very old age.'

Whitfield's disastrous incumbency does not seem to have permanently hurt the church, as when Revd Richard Polwhele published his three-volume account of Devon, he had this to say of Bideford in the second volume published in 1793:

Though the church be large enough to accommodate at least two thousand persons, yet, be it spoken to the honour of the inhabitants of this town, in an age when the very appearance of the religious character is too generally contemned, there is seldom, if ever, any reason to complain of the want of a large congregation every Sunday. Even the weekly prayer days, and the fasts and the festivals of the church, are certain of being properly respected here; and on such occasions, there is frequently a much larger congregation than in some churches is to be seen on a Sunday.

In the nineteenth century the interior of St Mary's was said to have become 'so disfigured by galleries and unsightly pews that it was deemed impossible to restore it.' It was therefore demolished, with the exception of the tower, and rebuilt in 1862–65 by a local builder, E.M. White, at a cost of £5,250, although his original tender was £3,758.

The reopening ceremony took place on 12 January 1865 and the *North Devon Journal* paid a glowing tribute to White and the architect Mr Ashwater, reporting:

Taking into consideration the excellence of the materials used, the elegance of the design and the beauty of the finish, together with its substantiality, and comparing this with the exceedingly moderate cost of erecting so handsome a fabric, any praise we could bestow would but ill reward these gentlemen.

The Bishop of Jamaica (standing in for the Bishop of Exeter) consecrated the building, assisted by 57 other clergymen in front of a huge congregation – some of whom provided the models for the carved heads decorating the outside of the new church. One of these was an unflattering representation of a 'crusty customer' who had annoyed the sculptor!

The new church was welcomed by everyone, although some inhabitants were annoyed that gravestones in the churchyard had been 'rooted up' to accommodate the new building. Burials had been stopped some years before, owing to overcrowding, but no map was produced to show where the graves had been located.

In 1881 a prefabricated iron church was erected to serve the growing population of East-the-Water. One story says it was paid for by a wealthy lady, who took her church to Ilfracombe when she moved, but the 'official' version seems more likely – that it was given to the vicar there when St Peter's Church, with 300 sittings, replaced it on the Barnstaple Street site in 1889.

A few years later, in 1906, Bideford became the centre of the battle between the so-called 'high' and 'low' wings of the Church of England when three 'low' Church preachers attended a service in St Mary's and then harangued the congregation as it left, accusing the then rector, Revd Leeke, of 'idolatorous practices'. The congregation and churchwardens proceeded to knock the men down and attempt to bodily throw them over the churchyard railings. The men were later charged with 'riotous behaviour' but the case was dismissed. This historic 'split' has occasionally resurfaced and arguments within the Church occurred even at the end of the twentieth century – but the Church continues to attract healthy congregations and provide a centre for worship, baptisms, marriages and funerals.

In 1757, John Wesley recorded in his journal:

Monday 3 October. I rode to Bideford but did not reach it until after five, the hour appointed for my preaching: so I began without delay in an open part of the street, where we alighted. One man made a little noise at first, but he was easily silenced: all the rest (a large number) quietly attended, though the wind was piercing cold, while I opened and applied 'God forbid that I should glory save in the cross of our Lord Jesus Christ.'

Although Methodists had been reported in Bideford in 1744, ministers were not appointed until 1788. A few years later it was said that the numbers were 'very small, with little or no prospect of increase.' Loiterers at the door of the 'preaching house' disturbed evening services by shouting, groaning and letting loose sparrows, which flew to the candles and put them out. In spite of such petty persecution more people joined, including prominent townsmen with money and energy to devote to the cause. The Chapel Street building, opened in or before 1816, soon had to be enlarged, and the inaugural service in 1834 was attended by over 1,300 people. In 1844, a breakaway group, the Bible Christians, opened their own chapel in Silver Street,

Above: *A view of the bells of St Mary's prior to rehanging in 1929.* (BL)

Left: *The site of the Methodist church in High Street prior to its construction as a Bible Christian chapel. The demolition of an old malthouse that existed on the site must have given the chapel-goers much satisfaction!*

Below: *The bells of St Mary's before their rehanging in 1929. They were taken down and recast by John Taylor & Son Ltd.* (BL)

Above: *The Bible Christian chapel in Silver Street was built in 1844 and, after later serving as a glove factory and a snooker hall, was demolished in 2004. This photograph from April of that year shows it just before the final destruction.* (PC)

Right: *The Temperance Hotel in Mill Street stood where the Baptist church stands at the time of writing. It harks back to a period when teetotalism was a lot commoner than in the twenty-first century.* (BL)

Right: *Some old cob-built buildings in High Street being demolished, c.1900, prior to their replacement by new brick-built houses. This reflects the new availability of imported building materials via the railway.* (BL)

Below: *The new houses being constructed – they still exist at the time of writing, although the houses to the right have gone and been replaced by the new Methodist chapel.* (BL)

Below right: *The Town Mission in Lime Grove dates from 1893 and is seen here at a time before the adjoining terrace was built and prior to the chapel's enlargement.* (PC)

The 'flying angel' tops the Seamen's Bethel in Torrington Street, East-the-Water, founded in 1877. (PC)

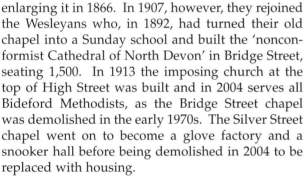

The Salvation Army Citadel used to stand in Honestone Street and was known as Island House, but was demolished in the 1980s to widen the road. A seventeenth-century drinking mural was discovered in the basement and removed to the Burton Art Gallery and Museum. (AB), (BB)

enlarging it in 1866. In 1907, however, they rejoined the Wesleyans who, in 1892, had turned their old chapel into a Sunday school and built the 'nonconformist Cathedral of North Devon' in Bridge Street, seating 1,500. In 1913 the imposing church at the top of High Street was built and in 2004 serves all Bideford Methodists, as the Bridge Street chapel was demolished in the early 1970s. The Silver Street chapel went on to become a glove factory and a snooker hall before being demolished in 2004 to be replaced with housing.

In 1818 a group of Baptist leaders came to the town to 'ascertain if there was an opportunity of commencing a Baptist cause.' A malt shop in Mill Street was hired as a temporary chapel, served fortnightly by the Barnstaple minister. In April 1821 the first adult baptisms took place in the Torridge but, within four years, 'owing to the small number of members and its disorderly state through lack of discipline,' the group disbanded. Three years later they started up again, in a coal cellar in Honestone Street! By 1837 they had built a chapel in Lower Gunstone, then a haunt of prostitutes and thieves. With a secure meeting-place the sect flourished and in 1866 erected some schoolrooms next to the chapel, which was enlarged two years later to provide 520 places, and further enlarged in 1898. The site was later carefully developed as a Baptist housing scheme, when the old chapel was replaced by the church in Mill Street.

Quakers came early to Bideford and are known to have set up a Meeting House, but this has since disappeared, and there were Plymouth Brethren in the town by July 1849, when nine people were

publicly baptised in the Torridge. An advertisement in the local newspaper shows that in 1855 they occupied a room in the building at the corner of High and Mill Streets. They later built a chapel in North Road which is still in use at the time of writing, although the building has been much altered. H.M. Restarick, shipbuilder and temperance man, was closely associated with the Seamen's Bethel, founded at East-the-Water in 1877 and enlarged 11 years later. Bideford also has a Town Mission in Lime Grove (1893), provision for Spiritualists in Hart Street, and a new 'outreach' group in Lower Meddon Street. Jehovah's Witnesses used to meet in the Market Place before building their own hall at Northam.

In 1882 a Roman Catholic priest from Barnstaple hired two rooms in the Music Hall in Bridgeland Street and fitted them up as a chapel. Nine years later building began on the site in North Road and the Church of the Sacred Heart was opened in December of that year. French Ursuline nuns established a convent in the town in 1904, but were replaced in 1929 by the Sisters of Charity. When the Roman Church returned more than 300 years after the Reformation, a wave of anti-Catholic feeling was set off in the still-puritanical town, but this soon died away and in the early-twenty-first century there is toleration for people of all creeds – and of none.

In a town where people endured much for freedom of religion in the past, words written of one local church at the end of the eighteenth century still apply to many of the congregations: '... once very numerous... [and] now... respectable... not only in point of members but of religion.'

Chapter 13

Good Learning

A plaque displayed in Bideford College shows that its 'ancestor', the Grammar School, was rebuilt in 1686 'to ye Glory of God and incouragement of Good Learning.' Before the Reformation, education had been the province of the Church; thereafter the main responsibility for 'good learning' devolved upon the Corporation and the Bridge Trust, until the arrival of state education.

A lease of 1617 which mentions 'The great seller under the School house', shows that the Grammar School existed by that time, but no earlier details have survived. It then consisted of one room about 60 feet by 25, in a building fronting Allhalland and Bridge Streets. It was refounded at the end of the century, after Mistress Susannah Stucley bequeathed £200 for the purpose, stipulating that the town should raise another £400. The target was exceeded by £20 and, in 1695, Richard Robertes of Bideford was appointed to teach 'the Lattin, Greek and Hebrew tongues' to six poor children and as many fee-paying pupils as he could attract, at an initial salary of £20 a year. 'Contributors' who had given money to the new foundation paid only half fees for their children – a 'perk' enjoyed by their descendants until 1803. The old building was still in use in the 1820s, for a pupil of that time recalled that the stocks, kept in a corridor beneath the Bridge Hall next door, 'were frequently used by the big boys against the little chaps.' The school moved for a time to Bridgeland Street, where the trustees had bought a house for the master, and in 1851 21 boarders aged from nine to 17, from places as far away as India and Jamaica, lived there. The master now received £50 per year and was allowed an assistant for every 30 additional scholars. In 1868 a new headmaster, finding the building 'Insanitary and incommodious', moved to Edgehill House in Northdown Road and changed the school's name to Bideford College. The move was unsuccessful until 1879, when a new head was appointed and new buildings erected in Northdown Road to house the 32 pupils then enrolled. Here the school stayed for the next 49 years.

In the seventeenth century, teachers had to be licensed by the Bishop, except during the Commonwealth when Bideford nonconformists, having rebuilt the Grammar School in 1657, appointed their own schoolmasters. After the Restoration two continued to teach, to the great annoyance of the licensed master who complained, 'I can use noe necessary discipline in my schole but presently they run from mee to one of them.'

The buildings at the end of the bridge looking up Bridge Street. Those to the right housed the original Bideford Grammar School, with the town stocks being kept in the covered walkway on the ground floor! (PC)

Parental (or pupil) choice thus began early in Bideford, where it was now also possible to achieve literacy without Latin. As early as 1625 an application for a licence had been made on behalf of William Parsons, who could not only teach writing, but was:

... skillful in the Art of Arithmeticke, very fitt and necessary to teach in this our towne of Bydeford being a towne of Navigation where such a one is to be imployed for the instructing and teaching the Children and printices [apprentices] of the inhabitance of our towne...

Arithmetic and navigation continued to be important subjects in Bideford and in the eighteenth century, George Donn, who kept a private school, and his sons Abraham and Benjamin, who taught there, were outstanding mathematicians. Benjamin's works included a volume of mathematical essays and a remarkable large-scale map of Devon, printed in 1765 from his own survey. There were many other private schools in Bideford by this time, both for boys and girls. Peter Glubb paid up to £3 a year for his daughters' schooling, and as much again for their dancing lessons. Lower down the social scale there were 'poor women to teach Little Children to Read' for a penny or two, and after 1761 even paupers' children were taught arithmetic, navigation, reading and writing in a 'Commercial' school founded by the Bridge Trust for 'ten... children either Boys or Girls, six of which to be taken from the workhouse and four from the poorer families of Bideford.' This school continued until 1878, and in the nineteenth century, there was also a school within the workhouse itself.

Left: *The British School in Higher Gunstone looking a bit worse for wear in 1985. Since being refurbished ownership has passed to Devon County Council, who run it as a Day Centre.* (PC)

Below: *The gallery seats and desks at the British School in Higher Gunstone.* (NDRO)

Bottom: *Architect's drawings of Bideford's British School. Monitors taught groups of younger children, who were expected to 'toe the line' (the 'U' shapes on the right of the schoolroom plan).* (NDRO)

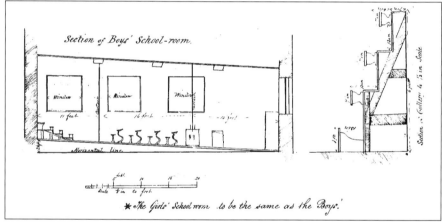

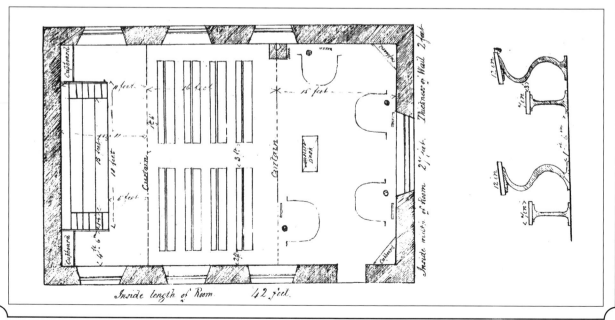

After 1800 schools for the poor were built all over the country, both by the Church of England's National Society founded by Andrew Bell, and Joseph Lancaster's rival British and Foreign Schools Society which, although non-denominational, mainly attracted nonconformists. Bideford's National School, known at first as Bell's School, was built in Old Town in 1823 and was supported by donations, church collections, balls and small fees. This provided 200 places for both boys and girls. The head teacher received £30 a year, a free house and coal. The Bridge Trust, showing no sectarianism, contributed to both the National School and the British School, which was opened in Higher Gunstone in 1836 for another 200 pupils. Both operated on the monitorial system, where the teacher taught a group of older children, who then instructed the younger ones. The system, although 'one of mass production in education', was better than nothing. Rivalry between the two societies continued, but the state, which was making grants to both, gradually began to regulate elementary education.

Parliament ordered a survey of all schools in England in the 1830s and published the results in 1835. The Bideford entry is intriguing and shows, by the number of schools available, just how important Bidefordians saw education. The enormous upsurge in establishments in the first few decades of the nineteenth century should also be noted.

BIDEFORD Parish (Pop.4,846.)
Twenty-nine Daily Schools: one of which contains 30 males, 3 of whom are free; the remainder are educated at the expense of their parents; this School is endowed with an estate, which lets for 56£ per annum, and a dwelling-house for the residence of the master: in another are 30 males, of these 10 are paid for by a salary of 10£ per annum, given by the feoffees of the Long Bridge Charity, the rest are paid for by their parents; in another (commenced since 1818) are 12 females; in another (commenced 1820) 6 males and 20 females; in another (commenced 1822) 2 males and 14 females; in another (commenced 1824) 38 males and 10 females; in two others (commenced 1824) 12 males and 20 females; in another (commenced 1829) 28 males and 7 females; in another (commenced 1830 10 females; in three others (commenced 1831) 45 males and 51 females (including 12 evening scholars of each sex); in another (commenced 1832) 6 females; in two others (commenced 1833) 26 males and 10 females; the remaining thirteen are small Schools for very young children, and contain 73 males and 112 females. In all the above Schools, with the exception of the two first mentioned, the children are instructed wholly at the expense of their parents.
One Day and Sunday National School (commenced 1823) containing 119 males and 102 females; this school was built at the sole expense of the feoffees of the Long Bridge Charity, and is supported by subscription

and by a collection after an annual sermon; the master has a salary of 40£, and the mistress 20£ per annum.
Two Sunday Schools: whereof one consists of 114 males and 105 females, and is connected with Independents; the other, of 165 males and 187 females, with Wesleyans; the former School has an endowment of 2£ per annum; excepting this, both Schools are supported by contributions, and have lending Libraries attached.

The Education Act of 1870 decreed that local school boards should be set up, with elected members and funding from the rates. After a stormy beginning, with charges of illegal electoral practices, the Bideford Board settled down to its work, which was to provide school places for all children between the ages of five and 12. The first state school was built in Torrington Lane, East-the-Water in 1874, to house 180 pupils, and the National and British Schools also became 'Board' schools. The population continued to rise and in the 1880s, when elementary education became compulsory, the National School was enlarged to include 250 places for girls and 300 for infants. Public money meant public inspection and a report on these schools in 1892 showed what was expected, and what was (or was not) achieved:

Girls' School – The girls are orderly but inattentive in class and too much disposed to prompt and talk to one another. Reading, Spelling and Recitation have fallen off and there seems no advance in general intelligence. On the other hand Writing and Arithmetic are better than they were. The Reading of the fourth standard was exceptionally bad. English has improved, but the needlework tests except in the fifth standard were not above fair.
Infants' School – in excellent order and remarkably well taught. The lowest class consisting of over 100 children is very much crowded.

In 1892 the ceiling of the upper-storey classroom of the Higher Gunstone school collapsed onto 80 infants sitting at their desks – but, amazingly all survived as, being small they 'slipped or were knocked under the desks and forms and thus, though well-nigh smothered and horribly frightened, they were not crushed.' Rebuilding began immediately as the available accommodation was already badly stretched. Indeed building could not keep up with population. The first infants' school, with 120 places, had been built in 1845 by subscriptions from church members on land on the corner of Honestone and High Street given by the Bridge Trust, and in 1883 another had been opened in Church Walk to provide an extra 165 places.

One pupil who attended the school in Higher Gunstone just prior to the First World War recalled the large classes that were the norm – although there was a smaller one used to isolate those children who had communicable diseases such as ringworm.

A locally-produced postcard showing the Church Infants' School at the top of Honestone Street. In 2004 the building houses the Angling Club. (LM)

Right: *An Infants' School was behind these buildings in Lower Meddon Street, with its 'playground' on the roof of the building on the left.* (PS)

Left: *Queen Street, c.1920, showing the building that, in the mid-nineteenth century, housed the Queen Street House Academy, a private school. In the early-twenty-first century it stands derelict.* (PC)

Right: *West Bank School in the 1940s. In 1955 it was moved to Sidmouth and the buildings were later taken over by Grenville College.* (PC)

Left: *As pupil numbers at West Bank School increased more room was needed, so these four houses in Lime Grove were acquired for use as 'The Senior Annexe'.* (PC)

As he noted, 'Once they got into that class they rarely came out.'

As we have seen already from the 1835 Parliamentary Report, private schools in Bideford flourished in the nineteenth century. In the 1820s, for example, young gentlemen could attend Mr Pickard's School in Allhalland Street, and their sisters the School for Young Ladies run by the Misses Luxmoore in Bridgeland Street – possibly the fore-runner of the school which, until the late 1920s, was held in what has since become the GB Revolution public house. Children under nine could be educated at the private infants' school run by Madame Pinckney in High Street. For those wanting a boarding-school there was a choice between Miss Martin's Mount Pleasant Establishment for the Board and Education of Young Ladies, and the Waterloo House Academy in the Strand under Charles Blackwell, to whom in 1839 the pupils presented a silver cup worth six guineas as a sign of their appreciation. Both buildings still exist as private houses at the time of writing.

Several well-known private schools flourish in Bideford in 2004. In 1884 the Bible Christians opened Edgehill College, a girls' secondary school. It had 42 pupils by the end of its first year and survived an outbreak of fever in 1887, and a devastating fire in 1920. An early prospectus made its aims clear:

The thoroughly genuine religious atmosphere and high moral standard maintained in the everyday life and associations of the girls cannot fail to exert a powerful and wholesome effect in the establishment and build-ing up of a noble character.

Discipline was firm, but not spartan, although in winter the girls sometimes had to break the ice in their water jugs before washing. The Stella Maris School, founded in 1929, was the 'descendant' of another convent school started in 1904 at Northdown House by Ursuline nuns, with the emphasis on 'ladylike manners, the French language and needlework.' A few years ago the school was amalgamated with Grenville College. Grenville was founded as a boys' school and has grown considerably since taking over the buildings of West Bank School, which was moved to Sidmouth in 1955. West Bank was founded in Lansdowne Terrace in 1896, as a private secondary and preparatory school, and later occupied various buildings in Abbotsham Road and Belvoir Hill. For a few years it had a companion boys' school, known as North Bank, in North Road.

For the state-school majority, the twentieth century brought more Education Acts, and for many years there was continued pressure on school places. In 1903, to relieve the desperately crowded Old Town buildings, Geneva Place School was opened to take 1,000 girls and infants. After the 1944 Act it became a secondary modern school. Meanwhile, the Grammar School, which had been taken over by the county council in 1928, had moved into new buildings in nearby Abbotsham Road, so it was possible to amalgamate the two in 1975 to form Bideford (Comprehensive) School.

The school in Old Town, which by 1926 was providing accommodation for 440 children, completely burnt down in that year. Sadly all the old school registers, its collection of silver trophies and some 300 photographs of old boys who had fought in the First World War were destroyed. In 2004 the site houses the Bideford Fire Station – a very apt use perhaps.

In 1854, Charles Kingsley 'seeing the young men of the town hanging about wasting their leisure hours,' started a free drawing class, of which Edward Capern, Bideford's postman-poet, became a member. The first official move towards education beyond school-leaving age came with the foundation of the Municipal Science, Art and Technical School in 1875, in what is, at the time of writing, the Freemasons' building in Bridgeland Street. In 1884 it was moved to the newly-erected Bridge Buildings on the Quay, and finally came to rest in its purpose-built home on the Pill in 1896. In the early-twenty-first century, full-time pupils having been transferred to Barnstaple, the building is, appropriately, a centre for adult education and evening classes.

New primary schools have replaced the Board schools, some of which have since been demolished. However, although used for other purposes, a number of old school buildings remain to remind new generations of the educational endeavours of the past.

'Kiltrasna' in the grounds of Edgehill College still provides accommodation for the students at the time of writing. (LM)

Centre and above left and right: *A selection of three postcards showing interior views of Edgehill College, c.1905 – it is clear that the premises were fairly spartan. Presumably the girls sent the cards home to reassure their parents about where they were living.* (LM)

Above: *The reopening of Edgehill College following a devastating fire in 1920. The builder's sign is for Ellis & Son of Mill Street.* (PC)

Right: *A biology class at Edgehill College, c.1949.* (NDJ)

Left: *This* North Devon Journal *photograph from March 1954 shows 'Boy Printers' at Bideford Secondary Modern School.* Left to right: *Brian Peake, Colin Faulkner and Tony Lavers. They are printing tickets in the school's printing class for the annual concert.* (NDJ)

One of the many private schools that flourished in Bideford, the Ursuline Convent became the Stella Maris School in 1929. (PC)

Right: *Still recognisable in 2004, the exterior of the old Art School on the Quay is decked out with flags and foliage, possibly to celebrate Queen Victoria's diamond jubilee.* (NDMT)

Below: *The highly-regarded head of the Bideford School of Art, James Paterson, making stained glass in September 1955.* (NDJ)

Left: *Part of Benjamin Donn's notable map of Devon which was engraved and published in 1765. Donn taught for a while in his father's private school in Bideford.*

Right: *The Board School in Geneva Place, c.1955. It was built in 1903 and in 2004 houses part of Bideford College.* (PC)

Below: *The newly-built Board School in Geneva Place looms large over a small selection of its scholars, c.1900.* (LM)

A selection of four photographs showing the interior of the Bideford Gazette *office in Grenville Street in 1935. They show (clockwise from top) the printing works with A. Saunders on the telephone, one of the finishing rooms the stationery shop at the front of the building and the printing press.* (PC)

Chapter 14

Historians and the Printed Word

A whole chapter on Bideford printers and writers and their products may seem excessive, but any historian must rely on them for much of their raw material – especially so in Bideford where there has been so little archaeological excavation and where so many manuscript records have disappeared. Having said this it is perhaps odd that Bideford was the first town in North Devon to have a history written about it. This was due to John Watkins who published his *An Essay towards a History of Bideford in the County of Devon* in 1792.

Watkins was apparently born in Bideford on 6 August 1765, being baptised in St Mary's 18 days later. His parents were Richard and Grace Watkins and he was the third of their four sons to be baptised there. The family had been resident in the town at least since 1730 when John's grandfather married in St Mary's. Although baptised into the Church of England we next find him being educated at Bristol for the nonconformist ministry. Evidently this did not last long as the same source states that he became 'dissatisfied' in 1786 and re-entered the established Church. His first career was in teaching at a school in Devon, possibly in Bideford, as in 1789 he published the sermons of Revd James Harvey who had been curate in the town from 1738 to '42. Three years later he published his history of Bideford. The reason why he collected this material is given in his preface where he states that it 'originated in the intention of giving some small assistance to the present ingenious historian of Devonshire.' This presumably refers to Revd Polwhele who published his three-volume *History of Devonshire* over the years 1793–1806. The list of subscribers shows that he sold a healthy 229 copies. Original copies are now scarce, although a second edition was published in 1883 and a third in 1993. Around 1794 Watkins is thought to have moved to London where he obtained a law degree and, as Dr Watkins, published many books on history and biography. When he died is not known although he was voted a pension of £30 per year by the National Benevolent Institution in November 1838, payment of which ceased, presumably with his death, in 1841.

Two further references to him are of some interest. In June 1852 J. Wilson, a printer and bookseller of Bideford, wrote to one of his customers about some local material he had in his possession, adding, 'I send also for your perusal, Doctor Watkins's Manuscript Prospectus for a History of Bideford' which reads:

Preparing and nearly ready for publication the History, Antiquities and Topography of the Town and Neighbourhood of Bideford in the County of Devon. Giving a descriptive account of all the Towns, Villages, Seats, and Curiosities, lying between the source of the Torridge and its Estuary; and from thence to the promontory of Hartland, by John Watkins LL.D. In the year 1792 the author printed a small volume entitled An Essay Towards A History of Bideford. As the impression run was small, copies have long become rare and scarcely obtainable. Besides this the work being a mere sketch, is deficient in many points of historic record and by the improvement that has since taken place it is now almost obsolete.

Sadly this manuscript was never published and appears to have been lost.

The second reference comes from an anonymous writer who, in 1858, noted:

There are two histories of Bideford, the first is now very rarely to be met with, indeed only two copies have ever come within my recollection. It is supposed to have been the produce of a Mr Donne formerly a schoolmaster here. The other a much later one was written in 1792 by Dr Watkins, a native of this place who went to London in early youth and there found employment in literary studies writing for the press. His work is generally acknowledged to be incomplete in every respect and... many persons... have expressed their wonder where the information was obtained from, in consequence of the limited nature of the public documents and these few not having been open to Mr Watkins's inspection. But it appears that much of his labour was lessened by the previous work of Mr Donne, one copy of which was in the possession of Mr George Buck of Daddon, to whom Watkins's book is dedicated and is now at Moreton. As a literary production the late work is a complete failure and a deal of matter had better been omitted, though a quantity of sound information is to be gathered from his pages.

Not a very good critical notice perhaps but Donn's book has disappeared, if it ever existed outside of manuscript, and we must be thankful to Watkins for producing his history.

Benjamin Donn (the usual spelling) was baptised in St Mary's on 22 June 1729, the last of six children born to George and Elizabeth Donn. George was parish clerk of Bideford from 1721 until at least 1745 and in addition ran a private school in the town.

Benjamin appears to have become a teacher in his father's school in his late teens and became locally renowned after publishing various papers in *The Mathematical Repository* and the *Gentleman's Magazine*. In October 1755 the latter of these two magazines published his long account of some aspects of the history of Bideford which we republish as Appendix I. This was illustrated by an engraving of the bridge which had been surveyed by his father. Watkins later reprinted George's meticulous measurements and, seemingly, identified Benjamin as the author of the unsigned *Gentleman's Magazine* article. Benjamin's most famous achievement was his map of Devon published in 1765 after six years of hard labour.

Bideford had to wait another 91 years after Watkins's effort before it was the subject of another history. In 1883 the Revd Roger Granville, rector of St Mary's, published a small volume entitled *The History of Bideford*. It drew heavily on Watkins as the author noted:

Unfortunately, a great number of old deeds and papers, relating both to the town and church of Bideford, were destroyed some years ago, which doubtless contained much interesting information, so that in undertaking to compile a history of Bideford I have had serious difficulties to labour under.

Heavily biased towards Church history and accounts of local landed families, the most interesting chapter is the final one on 'Modern Bideford', items from which have been used in this book.

In 1895 A. Inkerman Rogers issued a tiny booklet of just eight pages entitled *A Summary of the History of Bideford*. Inkerman, as he was always known, was son of William whose photograph appears in Chapter 11. He was a watchmaker and amateur geologist whose incredibly neat handwriting is instantly recognisable once you have seen it. His *Summary* is in the form of a chronological survey of the town from 1878 until 1894. It was reissued in 1937 having been extended to 40 pages in the interval. In addition, he published various other pamphlets on local topics including *Ships and Shipyards of Bideford 1568 to 1938* in 1947.

The next writer to tackle the town's history was W.H. Rogers (no relation to Inkerman) of Orleigh Court in Littleham who compiled a three-volume typescript *Notes on Bideford* which is dated 1939. This consisted of a series of short pieces on various aspects of the town's past. It was never written up as a proper book but it does contain many fascinating pieces of information.

W.H. Rogers of Orleigh Court, Littleham near Bideford, photographed in around 1935. Not only an historian of Bideford, he was also a local magistrate. (BL)

Rogers died in 1944 leaving the copyright of his work to Exeter University who chose not to publish it.

Some 14 years later Major W. Ascott published his oddly titled *Random notes on old Bideford and District –* which was exactly that. A small paperback, its charm lay in the recollections by its author of life in Victorian and Edwardian Bideford. His father had been landlord of the New Inn and a one-time Mayor of the town, whilst he himself was a long-serving secretary of the Bideford Horse Show and member of the Regatta Committee. He was also a churchwarden at St Mary's, a local magistrate and a Bridge Trustee.

In 1968 E. Muriel Goaman, who was the first female Mayor of Bideford under her married name of Cox, published *Old Bideford and District*. A slim volume only ever issued in paperback, it is a very useful history which is notable for the first appearance in book form of many of the now classic historical photographs of Bideford. Three more editions of this book have been published, the last as recently as 2003. Mrs Cox was even more well-known as the author of a series of books for children.

Another female writer on Bideford is Pat Slade who followed Mrs Cox's lead and published a very evocative collection of photographs of old Bideford under the simple title *Bideford*. She is the long-standing chair of the Bideford and District Community Archive set up under a 1980s Manpower Services Commission scheme by Frank Gent with assistance from Peter Christie.

Much of W.H. Rogers' material appeared in *A History of Bideford* by Duncan Fielder which was published in 1985. The best feature of this book is the series of drawings by Jim Paterson, the last head of the Bideford School of Art on the Quay and a noted craftsman in stained glass.

In 1987 the authors of *The Book of Bideford* published an earlier version of this book – the first volume to provide a reasonably complete history of the town. Sadly the publishers went bankrupt not long after publication, and so copies quickly became scarce. Since its publication Alison Grant has gone on to publish much new material on the Bideford potters and the early trade of the town, whilst Peter Christie has continued to publish his weekly column on local history in the local newspaper. Both of these sources have been extensively drawn on to produce *The Book of Bideford* which hopefully takes its place as the standard history of the town.

The presence of writers presupposes an audience and a market for their writings. Literacy only became general following the Education Act of 1870 but even before this date various booksellers and

Right: *Mill Street showing the office of the* Western Express *newspaper with the still-existing statue of the 'Ragged Newsboy' on top. The newspaper began in 1886.* (PC)

Above: *Fluck & Co.'s book and stationery shop in the High Street in around 1900. Three doors down is Harper's Library and Bookshop.* (BL)

Left: *Inkerman Rogers in a photograph from one of his own publications –* John Rogers, Proto-Martyr, *which was published in 1944.* (PC)

Left and below: *A partial list of 'Pamphlets, Monograms and Contributions' by Inkerman Rogers. It is written in his own hand.* (PC)

publishers were to be found in Bideford. The earliest we have any record of is Mrs Jane Manning, a bookseller who was advertising in the *Exeter Flying Post* in 1763. Doubtless she also sold the newspaper as well as books and stationery from her premises. She was succeeded by M. Manning whose ornate sale sticker has been preserved in a book dating from 1801.

These pioneers were joined by many others and a few are dealt with here. Around 1791 Thomas Griffiths set up a bookshop in Barnstaple and married there before moving to Bideford aged around 27. He seems to have prospered, adding printing to his bookselling business and becoming the owner of at least three properties in the town before his death in 1806. The business was carried on by his widow Anne with two of their 12 children, Thomas and Anne, who eventually took it over – whilst another son Benjamin became a local printer. Thomas junr ran a shop in High Street for many years where he sold patent medicines as well as books and stationery. The Griffiths dynasty had been joined in 1796 by John Handford who opened a 'Circulating Library', probably in the High Street where members paid a small fee to read the latest books. This was the town's first recorded library although its life appears to have been rather short as references to it are rare.

Some time around the opening years of the nineteenth century Robert Wilson moved to Bideford from Torrington and established his printing shop on the Quay. He died in 1834 but had already taken his son John into the business and he was publishing material under his own name by 1829. That he was a successful businessman is shown by the fact that he added ship brokering and printing to his basic bookselling activities. According to W.H. Rogers he published the *Western Standard* for a few months in 1852, along with the short-lived *Bideford Gazette* in 1854 – the town's first newspapers. The latter was roughly A4 in size and consisted of four pages and lasted just four issues. The business passed to his sons and was still operating in Mill Street as late as 1926.

Around 1820 William Cole established his bookshop and printing press in Allhalland Street from where he issued a wide variety of printed stationery, much of which was for the use of the Town Council. He also established a circulating library around 1828 and, as with other booksellers, his son later joined him in the business. William died in December 1875 and was buried in Old Town Cemetery.

A directory of 1830 lists Thomas Snell's bookshop in Emma (or Grenville) Street, his shop being at number six. Seven years later Thomas and a partner called Johnson sold the business to John Gould Hayman, the son of a Wesleyan minister who added printing and bookbinding services. Evidently he flourished, as in 1852 he became one of the joint proprietors of the Barnstaple-based *North Devon Journal* which had been established in 1824.

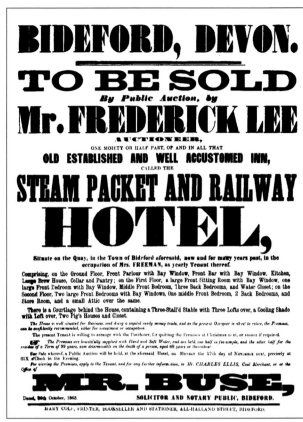

An example of the everyday print jobs undertaken by a Victorian printer – in this case Mary Cole of Allhalland Street, Bideford. (PC)

The business was sold to Thomas Honey in October 1853 and in January 1856 he began publishing the *Devon and East Cornwall Gazette and Commercial Advertiser*. This was a broadsheet newspaper of just four pages, three of which were bought in ready printed, with local news and advertisements being added by Honey on the remaining page. Within six months Thomas changed the rather ponderous title to one not much less wordy viz.: *The Bideford Weekly Gazette and Devon and Cornwall Advertiser*, although it was only ever known as the *Bideford Gazette*. Sadly Thomas died on 21 November 1856 aged 27 and was buried in Old Town Cemetery. His 25-year-old wife Eliza, having given birth to their first child five months before, decided to carry on the business, thus becoming possibly the only female newspaper editor in Victorian Britain. She eventually passed her interest in the paper on to a relative, W.H. Honey, in September 1875.

W.H. Honey sold the business in June 1882 to W. Crosbie Coles, who was later joined by a Mr Owen, although he soon left to be replaced by a Mr Lee. Following takeovers by increasingly distant owners, the *Gazette* became a tabloid in March 1983, leaving its Bideford base for Barnstaple a few years later and eventually dropping its Bideford links, becoming simply the *North Devon Gazette*. The *Gazette* was the only Bideford-based paper until around 1863, when

The Western Express was started by Thomas Tedrake from his office at 48 Mill Street. This was eventually swallowed up by the *Gazette* but its memory is perpetuated by the lifelike figure of a 'ragged newsboy' atop Tedrake's old office and shop.

Moving on to the twentieth century, a directory of 1930 lists just two printers and six stationers, one of whom, Sydney Harper, had a sizable stock of second-hand books. One of his competitors was Fluck & Co. Over the century printers and booksellers have come and gone so that for much of the late-twentieth century the book trade was represented by Mackenzie Dye in Mill Street and Discovery at various locations in the town. Although Mackenzie's has disappeared, two new shops have been established – Walter Henry's Bookshop, which is part of Chope's, and a second-hand shop in Allhalland Street. These are augmented by three printers; Kopykat, Polypress and Lazarus Publishing, who produce everything from advertising and political leaflets to fully-fledged books. In 2004 Bideford is well-supplied with both books and writers.

Left: A sale sticker from a book sold by M. Manning. The book itself was printed in 1801. It was usual for booksellers to sell patent medicines up until the late-nineteenth century. (NDRO)

Mrs E.M. Cox (née Goaman) who was Bideford's first female Mayor and author of many books including Old Bideford and District. (NDJ)

An advertisement from Perkin's Almanac of 1884 publicising the second edition of Watkins's History of Bideford. *The Almanac itself first appeared in 1876 and is now extremely rare.* (PC)

Above: The centenary of the Bideford Gazette *in 1954. Sadly, they were two years too early! Left to right: W. Harris (Chairman, Bideford RDC), T. Moore (President, Newspaper Society), George Lambert MP, C. Grant (Mayor of Bideford), J. Cruse (Deputy Mayor of Barnstaple), M.F. Lee (Managing Director,* Bideford Gazette*), John Heywood (Chairman Northam UDC), J. Lang (Mayor of Torrington).* (NDJ)

BIDEFORD, NORTH DEVON.

TO BE SOLD, by Public Auction, by Mr. FREDERICK LEE, at Maunder's 'Newfoundland Inn,' on Thursday, the 24th day of April instant, at 6 o'clock in the evening (if not previously disposed of by Private Contract, of which, due Notice will be given), the Fee-Simple and Inheritance of and in all that

DWELLING HOUSE AND BUSINESS PREMISES,

Situate in Grenville-street, in the Town aforesaid, now and for many years past in the occupation of Mrs. HONEY.

The House contains on the Ground Floor, Spacious Front Shop, with Two Windows, Parlour, Kitchen, Wash House, Offices, Court Yard, &c.; First Floor, a Large Sitting Room, Bed Room, and Linen Closet; Second Floor, Four Good Bedrooms, with Attic over. Leading from the Front Shop, and approached by Stairs is a Printing Office.

The Premises are well supplied with Hard and Soft Water, and conveniently fitted up with Cupboards, Grates, and Chimney Pieces.

The above offers an excellent opportunity to parties requiring a good Business Premises, being contiguous to the Market and principal thoroughfare in the Town, and for the past 50 years has been known (and occupied) as a Printing and Bookselling House.

☞ For further particulars, apply at the Office of the Auctioneer, or to Mr. ROOKER, Solicitor, *Bideford.*

Dated April 2nd, 1862. [5411

Left: A sale notice from the North Devon Journal *for the sale of the Grenville Street office of the* Bideford Gazette *in 1862. The premises remained as a printing works until around 1990.* (NDJ)

Conclusion

This book has attempted to tell the history of Bideford, including the many changes the town has experienced over the last 1,000 years. Such changes are always occurring – indeed it is sobering to catalogue just those changes that have happened in the last 20 years. The high-level Torridge Bridge and the associated bypass, plus the East-the-Water Relief Road, have both been built, whilst during 2004 the cliffs overhanging the road to Torrington were stabilised after a rock fall. Safeway (becoming Morrisons at the time of writing) and the Atlantic Village shopping complex have both come to Bideford along with new industry at Caddsdown and along the Alverdiscott Road – with the promise of more to come in both localities. In terms of houses, Londonderry Farm estate is nearly complete at the time of writing, whilst East-the-Water is set to accommodate another large new housing area to go along with the development at Eastridge Farm.

Old buildings have been successfully refurbished including the old Workhouse in Meddon Street, the Cafecino Plus, Crabby Dick's, Friendship House, the Pannier Market, the Old Bakery and Post Office Mews. The Burton Art Gallery and Museum was reopened in 1994 after a major extension and is one of the major cultural tourist attractions in the South West, as well as providing an ever-changing series of exhibitions for local people.

The Quay has, once again, been widened – this time by 18 feet to prevent both salt-water penetration and to counter the rise in sea level from global warming. Its rebuilding was not without rancour but most now agree that it has become a splendid addition to the town's landscape and hopefully will maintain Bideford's role as a port for many years to come.

The Kenwith Valley has become a registered nature reserve and even now moves are afoot to develop the old route of the Bideford, Westward Ho! and Appledore Railway, which runs along the valley, into an extension of the Tarka Trail. The Town Council are also trying to safeguard a 'green' corridor from Atlantic Village down to Jennet's reservoir to protect the town's unofficial 'green belt'.

Some things have gone, however – the Stella Maris convent school has disappeared and its buildings have been turned into flats, whilst the last shipyard in the town has closed and its site houses a large estate of riverside properties. The cinema has been knocked down, although a new one has replaced it at Bideford College. Many old shops have gone, although Chope's, Braddick's and the long-established public houses still flourish.

Looking back over the last two decades one can only be astonished at the sheer number of changes Bideford has gone through. Others are promised for the future. Alterations and repairs must be made to the old bridge, yet the current suggestions have not found much favour with the townspeople; Sure Start is to develop a large new centre in the town; and East-the-Water is to experience the largest growth it has ever known – including the possible development of a Higher Education Centre on the old Brunswick Wharf site.

All these changes, whether in the future or already here, have not come easily – yet we are convinced Bideford has become the better for them. The 'Little White Town' is no longer little, and few of its buildings are now whitewashed, yet it is still the small, friendly market town it has always been – and we have been proud to record its story here in the book you are now holding.

Peter Christie and Alison Grant, 2005

Flooding on the Quay in the 1950s. The new Quay flood defences should make this sight disappear, at least for 100 years – that being the design life of the scheme. (PC)

At the bottom of Cooper Street, c.1900. In 2004 the building to the right is Caesar's Palace, the largest nightclub in town – a good example of how the uses of buildings are constantly changed and updated. (BL)

An atmospheric 1950s photograph of part of the Quay. Note the decorative lights on top of the garage's famous 'dome'. The conjunction of a double-decker bus and the trees overhanging the road led to damaging collisions. The new trees on the Quay have been set back to avoid this. (LM)

August 2004 and the riverbed next to the bridge is being reinforced with concrete 'mattresses' to help defend it against scour from the fast-flowing river water. (PC)

Dingle's shop in Buttgarden Street was the second in on the right from Market Hill. Mr and Mrs Dingle, and a shop assistant, complete with aprons, pose proudly for the photographer in the 1920s. In the last 30 years such small grocery shops have been forced out of business by the large superstores. (LM)

The original Safeway store, c.1990, which stood opposite the site where the superstore stands at the time of writing. It began life as a branch of 'Prestos'. (BB)

Appendix I

Donn's account of Bideford, 1755

The first full account of Bideford and its history appeared in *The Gentleman's Magazine* for October 1755. According to a note in Watkins's 1792 book this was written by 'Mr Donne', although whether he means the father George or the son Benjamin it is unclear. Benjamin had, however, contributed a number of observations in previous years to the magazine, so it seems probable he was the author of the article reproduced below – and possibly also the 'Supplement' which appeared two months later.

Some Account of BIDDEFORD, in Answer to the Queries relative to a Natural History of England.

Biddeford was anciently written By-the-Ford, there having been a Ford just above the bridge, on a spot where an house is standing, called Ford-house.

It is situated on the sides of two hills, between which a fine river runs thro' it. Over this river is a bridge, and many errors have been propagated concerning both.

It has been said that the arches of the bridge are so wide and lofty, that vessels of 50 tons may sail thro' them; but tho' ships of much less burthen cannot sail thro', yet ships of much greater may go thro' without masts. It has also been said that the water runs quite out of the river at ebb, and that carts not being permitted to come on the bridge, take this opportunity to pass over on the sands: but this is wholly false, for at the lowest water there is a channel in the middle sufficient to float pleasure boats; and not only carts, but wagons of three tons weight are permitted to cross the bridge, upon paying an acknowledgement to the bridge warden. Some authors have asserted, that tho' the foundation of the bridge is firm, yet it will shake at the lightest tread of a horse; but this is also a mistake, for the foundation is immoveable, the arch indeed not being covered with a sufficient weight is so elastic, that it yields and springs up again under the rapid motion of a coach.

The boats used on the river for hire are passage boats, ballast boats, and lighters; in the passage boat a passenger is carried from Biddeford to Appledore, three miles for a penny, and the hire of a lighter that will carry 10 tons, for a whole tide, is 5s.

The town in general is well built, particularly a new street fronting the key, which is Bridge land, and inhabited by people of fortune. The key itself is in the body of the town, and so commodious that ships of 200 tons may lay their side to it, and unload without the

Steam and sail alongside the Quay in the interwar period. In the early-twenty-first century Bideford port gets fewer ships – but they are far larger. (LM)

The Quay in the late 1920s, showing that crowded parking bays are nothing new. The original frontage of what is Freebird cycle shop at the time of writing shows up well in this scene. (LM)

use of a lighter. It is a place of considerable trade, but the herring fishery has failed for some years, and so has the manufacturing rock salt into what was called salt upon salt, by first dissolving it in sea water, and then boiling it again. Great quantities of potters ware are made, and exported to Wales, Ireland, and Bristol.

The merchants of Biddeford lost almost all their vessels in the late French war, but by buying and building have again made up their number near 100, most of which now lie by, as the hands that should have navigated them were swept away by the press, and others cannot be procured.

It sends no member to parliament.

It is governed by a mayor, aldermen, recorder, capital burgesses, town clerk, sergeants etc and has a particular court, in which actions of debt, and upon the case, may be brought for any sum.

The Granvilles have been lords of this place ever since the conquest till very lately, and in the 11th year of Q. Anne, it gave the title of baron to George late lord Landsdown.

There is a market three days in a week, on Tuesdays, Thursdays, and Saturdays; the Tuesday's and Saturday's markets are most considerable; Tuesday's being well served with corn, and other provisions: Thursday's is called the little market, and is held in a different part of the town.

The price of provisions is very variable. Wheat is from 3s 6d to 10s per bushel; the common price is from 4s to 5s. Beef is from 2½d to 4d per pound; and butter from 3½d to 9d.

The number of houses is about 500, and allowing five persons to each house the number of inhabitants will be about 2500.

The church though it is large, and has two ayles and two galleries, can yet but just contain the number of persons that attend divine worship: great part of it has been lately new built; the whole has been repaired and beautified, and new seats have been made. It was first furnished with an organ about 25 years ago, and the organist's salary is 20£ per Ann. It has also a good ring of six bells, and the tower being near the river, the tone is rendered more soft and musical. The motto on the treble is, Peace and good neighbourhood, and that on the tenor, I to the church the living call, and to the grave I summon all.

The church is in the manor of Biddeford, the diocese of Exeter, the hundred of Shebeare, and the deanery of Hartland. The present rector is the Rev. Mr. John Whitfield, M.A. His predecessors were the Rev. Mr. Nichols, Dr. Herbert Bedford, and — Ogilby, who was chaplain in ordinary to king Charles II.

The living is worth 200£ per Ann. And the present patron is the Rt. Hon. the lord Gower.

There is an epitaph in the western wall of the church yard that fixes a point of chronology, and shews that the plague raged with great violence at Biddeford in 1646. The persons buried under it are three children of Henry Ravening, surgeon, who were the first that the disease carried off, and were supposed to contract it by playing on some bags of wool that were just landed on the key.

There are two dissenting meeting-houses, one of which is pretty large, the number of dissenters being computed to nearly 1-4th of the whole.

The parish register began in 1561, when there were no dissenters. The number of christenings for the first 20 years was 473, for the last 20 years 1151, so that the whole number of christenings for the last 20 years must be 1151, and 1-4th more, being nearly 1535. Marriages for the first 20 years were 114, for the last 20 years 395. The burials in the first 20 years were 255, and the last 1597.

There is a grammar school, endowed with about 20£ per ann.

About two miles down the river is a place called Hubblestone, from a large stone of the same name, of which they relate the following story. In the reign of king Alfred one Hubba, a Dane, having desolated South Wales with fire and sword, came to Appledore with 33 sail of ships, and landing his troops besieged the castle of Kenwith, but being opposed with great courage by the Devonshire men he was slain, and buried under this stone, to which they gave his name, and called it Hubba's-stone. In the Magna Brittania this castle is said to be at that time called Hennaborough, but I believe it to be the place now called Henny Castle, situated on a hill about a mile NW of Biddeford.

As to remarkable or illustrious persons, there is in the church, near the communion table, the monument of a warrior; he lies extended, is completely armed, and has a dog by him; on an arch that is turned over him is an inscription, which I read thus Hic jacet Thomas Grauntvild, miles patronus istius ecclesiae, obiit 15 in die mensis Martii, A.D. 1513, cujus animae propitiatur Deus. Amen. This gentleman was of the illustrious family of Granville, but nothing is known of him more than the inscription tells.

There is also a monument to Mr John Strange, an eminent merchant. The life of this gentleman was rendered remarkable by many incidents, that seemed as if he was brought into the world and preserved by providence for a particular purpose, which he lived to accomplish, notwithstanding several accidents that would otherwise have been fatal, and then died when it might reasonably have been expected that he would have had a longer life. When he was very young he fell from a very high cliff without receiving any hurt, and he was afterwards struck on the forehead by an arrow, which just raised the skin and glanced away, without doing him any farther injury. When the plague broke out in Biddeford the mayor deserted his trust, and fled the place; this was the crisis for which Mr Strange seems to have been born; he was chosen mayor instead of the fugitive, and during the whole time that the pestilence raged, he went into the infected houses, to see that the sick were properly attended, to prevent the houses of the dead from being plundered, and to see that the bodies were properly interred; after he had performed this good work, and there was none sick of the disease in the place, he sickened of it, and being the last that it destroyed, his death crowned his labours, and conferred his reward.

As to natural history. Biddeford is bounded to the north by Northam, to the north-east by Westley, to the south-east by Ware Giffard, to the south by Littleham, and to the west by Abbotsham. It is remarkable that though Northam is two miles north of Biddeford, yet part of the parish is a mile south of it.

The latitude of Biddeford is 51o 6' N. the longitude about 4o 15' west of London, from which it is distant about 200 miles.

The soil is hilly and rocky, with blackish mould, yellowish clay, fens, marsh, wood, arable, pasture, and heath. The chief product is wheat, barley, peas, and beans. There are many good quarries of hard, durable stone for building in the rocky part, and in the clay part very good earth for bricks. There is also a culm pit, which was worked for fuel a few years ago, when coal, which is usually sold for 1s per bushel, double Winchester, was very dear.

The principal manure is lime, ashes, dung, and sea sand, that in colour resembles unburnt umber, but is lighter and more yellow; a sea weed, called oarweed, is also sometimes used, but principally for gardens. The ashes are made by spading the turf from the surface of the ground, and then burning it in heaps.

The springs are generally found at the depth of about 16 feet, and the water is very sweet and soft, except near the key, and there it is a little brackish.

The air is in general healthy, tho' the place is frequently covered with thick fogs from the sea.

The Aurora Borealis is very common, and one was very singular, of which a particular account has already been given in Vol.XX p.270.

It is high water at the bridge at new and full moon about six o'clock, but sometimes the wind considerably alters the time: In stormy weather it has sometimes fallen about a foot after high water, and then risen again as high as before. If the wind blows strong at south west, a high spring tide seldom fails to overflow the key, and rise so high under the arches of the bridge, that the smallest boat cannot pass. A common spring tide, without the concurrence of a south-west wind, generally lays all the marshes under water.

As to wages day labourers have per diem 1s house-carpenters and masons 1s 6d ship-carpenters on old work 2s on new 1s 6d and the master 2s 6d.

In the bay, lat. 51. 14 N. lies the island of Lundy, which is five miles long and two broad, but so incompassed with rocks, that it is accessible only in one part, and the avenue there is so narrow, that a few men might defend this pass against a multitude. If to this natural fortification a small fort had been added, the petty French privateers who lurked there in queen Anne's war, to our great loss, might have been driven away. They took so many of our vessels, for which they lay in wait in this place, that they called it Golden Bay. But tho' no fort is yet built, yet the Bristol privateers so effectually protected the trade in this place, during the last war, that not a single vessel was taken. Wrecks are very frequent on the rocks about the bay, and a proposal was lately made to erect a lighthouse on Hartland point by a gentleman remarkable for public spirit, who offered, if this proposal was complied with,

What the occasion was is uncertain, but Bidefordians clearly liked flags! During 2004 the road width has been considerably reduced as part of modern 'traffic management'. (LM)

151

to erect a mathematical school in Biddeford, and endow it with 50£ per ann. No light-house is yet erected.

The island is four leagues distant from the nearest land, but it abounds with fine springs of fresh water. The soil in the southern part is good, but the northern part is rocky. There is, among others, one craggy, pyramidical rock, so remarkable for the number of rats boroughing about it, that it is called Rat Island. The whole island abounds with rabbits and wild fowl. It is said that no venomous creature will live upon it. It is inhabited by only one family, who sell liquors to such fishermen as put on shore there. It is said to be in the hundred of Branton and to be the property of Ld Gower.

On Northern Burroughs, which is distant from Biddeford about four miles below the bridge, there is a beach of pebbles, about three miles long, of very considerable breadth and depth, so that altho' they have been long used as ballast, the number is not perceptibly diminished. These stones are from 6 to 18 inches long, curiously variegated with veins of different colours, and sufficiently hard to take a fine polish; on the outside of them grows a great quantity of the Lichen marinus, or sea liverwort, which is much esteemed by the neighbouring inhabitants as a wholesome and pleasant food, being gently opening, and an antiscorbutic. It is frequently packed up in earthern pots and sent to London.

Of the places above bridge none are worth notice except Ware Giffard, which is also distant from Biddeford about four miles; at this place the water of the river first becomes fresh, and sometimes rises so suddenly, that the inhabitants on the key are not only confined to their houses, but driven to the upper rooms. The fish above bridge are trouts, gravelling salmon, flukes, flounders, eels, bass, and millet; and below rock, bass, cod, oysters, cockles, and muscles, tho' of the shell fish muscles only are plenty, the oysters being generally brought from Tenby in Wales,

and sold at about 1s per six score. Mackerel are also brought in their season by the Comb boats, and herrings from Clovelly in such plenty, as to be sometimes sold at the rate of seven for a penny.

In the parish of Fremington are great quantities of reddish potters clay, which are brought and manufactured at Biddeford, whence the ware is sent to different places by sea; And near Ware Giffard there is plenty of fine pipe-makers clay, many ship loads of which are annually exported to Bristol, Liverpool, Chester, and other places.

SUPPLEMENT TO THE ACCOUNT OF BIDDEFORD

Adjoining to Biddeford on the north is Raleigh, probably so called after some of the illustrious family of Sir Walter Raleigh. Just above the bridge is a little ridge of gravel of a peculiar quality, without which the potters could not make their ware. There are many other ridges of gravel within the bar, but this only is proper for their use, and for some particular purposes in masonry. This ridge is often washed away by the freshes, but always gathers again, exactly in the same place, as soon as they abate. About a mile above the bridge on the west is Lancras, said to be the birth place of general George Monk, afterwards duke of Albermarle. At a little more than three miles above the bridge, in the parish of Monkleigh, is Annery, said to be the birth place of Walter Stapledon, bishop of Exeter, and lord high treasurer of England.

About four miles from Biddeford, in the parish of Alwington, is a place called Yeo, now the seat of – Bruton, Esq; a very antient and handsome building. It is said to derive its name from a pleasant stream of water, which in French is called Eau, whence by corruption Yeau, and at last Yeo. At this place are the remains of a chapel, in which was a dormitory for the dead.

[In the inscription, p.447, for XV in die, read XVIII die, and for propitiatur, propitietur.]

The Quay near the end of the bridge, showing how much the area had been extended outwards since Donn wrote his account. During 2003 an extra 18 feet were added – an example of the continuity of history. (HC)

Appendix II

The Population of Bideford

This book has recounted the growth of Bideford in physical terms – the spread of buildings and developments in trade. This appendix examines the population changes as far as this is possible, bearing in mind that our ancestors were not as interested in statistics as we have become. The earliest source we can turn to is the parish register. First ordered to be kept by Henry VIII, parish registers generally began in 1538, although examples from this date are uncommon. Bideford's first surviving register dates from 1561. Until 1754 entries for baptisms, marriages and burials are mixed up together. Following Lord Hardwicke's Act for the Better Preventing of Clandestine Marriages in that year, marriage entries were recorded in separate books whilst burials were given their own volumes in 1813 following an Act of Parliament passed in the preceding year.

We can get a rough estimate of a settlement's population by adding up the total baptisms over a decade, working out the annual average and then multiplying this figure by 30. In Bideford's case this gives the following figures up to 1799 (the first four are based on figures given in Watkins's book)

1561–70	573
1570–80	879
1580–90	999
1590–1600	936
1600–09	1,077
1610–19	1,185
1620–29	1,665
1630–39	1,746
1640–49	1,779
1650–59	1,749
1660–69	1,668
1670–79	1,950
1680–89	2,610
1690–99	1,962
1700–09	1,860
1710–19	1,737
1720–29	1,782
1730–39	1,950
1740–49	1,635
1750–59	1,509
1760–69	1,512
1770–79	1,464
1780–89	1,938
1790–99	2,316

From these rough estimates it is clear that Bideford was a very small place in the sixteenth century, whilst the following century saw steady growth related to the expansion of the North American trade which reached a peak in the years 1680–89. From then on there appears to have been a fairly marked decline until the end of the eighteenth century. This, however, is probably more to do with the growth of nonconformism in the town and thus the absence of many baptisms from the registers as the new religious groups stopped going to St Mary's. It could also reflect the unpopularity of the town's Church of England vicars at this date *(see Chapter 12)*, which could well have driven parents to surrounding parishes to baptise their children. Sadly, the patchy survival of Bideford's nonconformist registers means we cannot give a detailed analysis of these listings to supplement the figures from the Church of England registers.

Other records exist, however, that can be used to estimate population totals. These include the Compton Return of 1676 which gives the numbers of male and female conformists, nonconformists and Roman Catholics over the age of 16 in each English parish. Bideford recorded a suspiciously rounded number of 2,500 conformists and just 96 nonconformists (with no Catholics). Using an accepted multiplier of 1.66 thus gives a population of 4,309 – more than double the figure we estimated using the parish register figures. This clearly shows how variable such population estimates can be – although again this might just reflect vested interests in those who compiled the figures.

Over the eighteenth century the Bishop of Exeter asked on four occasions how many families there were in each of the parishes in his diocese. Using another multiplier of either 4.75 or 6 (to allow for

Meddon Street with the Torridge Inn (since closed) facing the photographer. All the shops in this photograph have gone, but a new one has opened. For many centuries this area was the southern boundary of the town. (LM)

Milton Place, c.1900, before the building in the centre was cleared to widen access – clearly Bideford was not built for the car! (BL)

Looking up Chingswell Street some time in the 1920s. A large house once stood to the left but was demolished and the site used for new housing. The opportunity was also taken to widen the road – which was later completed for the whole length of the building. (BL)

variation in family sizes) we can calculate the following population totals:

1744 – between 2,375–3,000
1764 – between 2,375–3,000
1779 – between 3,800–4,800
1798 – between 2,470–3,120

These results again point to considerable under-recording of Bidefordians in the parish registers.

If these very variable totals are confusing we reach firmer ground in the nineteenth century when proper census results become available. The first such survey was taken in 1801 both to discover manpower resources available during the long-running Napoleonic Wars and to settle long-running Parliamentary arguments over whether the population was growing or shrinking. Since the first one a census has been taken every ten years, except for 1941 when the Second World War superseded the counting of the population. The figures were as follows:

1801 – 2,987
1811 – 3,244
1821 – 4,053
1831 – 4,846

1841 – 5,211
1851 – 5,775
1861 – 5,742
1871 – 6,969
1881 – 6,596
1891 – 7,875
1901 – 8,754
1911 – 9,078
1921 – 9,125
1931 – 8,778
1941 – X
1951 – 10,100
1961 – 10,498
1971 – 11,802
1981 – 12,210
1991 – 13,226
2001 – 14,675

The steady growth through the nineteenth century is clear, as is the effect of the First World War on the town. The slower growth at the end of the twentieth century was due to a halt in house building placed on the town by South West Water and Torridge District Council because of an overloaded sewerage system. This has now been lifted and Bideford is set to experience some long-constrained growth.

This extraordinary view from c.1900 shows Pitt Lane. On the left is the high wall (which is still standing) surrounding 'Iffield' and to the right is the first house in Lime Grove. For many years this land formed the western boundary to the town. (BL)

Above: *The demolition of existing houses and their replacement by a greater number of new houses is beginning to occur in Bideford. This photograph shows a Lime Grove bungalow occupied by Captain Beer, named 'Devonia' after his vessel, that was replaced by five houses in 1971.* (AB)

Right: *Towards the end of the nineteenth century and for the first decade of the twentieth Bideford saw a boom in house building as people began demanding better housing. Here we see the newly completed first terraced house in Abbotsham Road with the proud owner Rosa Cock standing outside.* (LM)

Subscribers

Roger Ackland, Bideford, Devon
Mike and Chrys Aitken, Bideford
Keith and Lorraine Anderson, Northam
Charles P. Anstis, Bideford, Devon
Ian T. Arnold, Bideford, Devon
John E. Ash, Bideford East, Devon
Colin Atkins, Bideford, Devon
Selena Atkins, Bideford, Devon
Suzanne Atkins, Bideford, Devon
Jean Atkinson, Bideford, Devon
F.A. Backhurst, Bideford, Devon
John R. Baker
Paul W. Baker, Exeter
Thomas Baker, Londonderry
Anthony and Julia Barnes, Bideford
D. Barnes, Bideford, Devon
Sahara Barton, Appledore, Bideford, Devon
M. Beaumont, Bideford
William E. Bedler, Bideford, Devon
Colin A. Beer, Bideford, Devon
D. Beim, Instow, Devon
Jane E. Bennett, Bideford
K. Bennett, Bideford, Devon
Philip R. Berry, Bideford, Devon
Mr V.C. and Mrs R.J. Berry, Bideford
Alan Bettiss, Bideford, Devon
Mr S.T.R. (Roy) Bird, Bideford
Ms Carolyn Blackmore, Bideford, Devon
Dr John Blackmore, Ealing, London
Ken and Elma Blackmore, Braunton, Devon
Mr Arthur Blamey
Brian W. Boland, Bideford, Devon
Clive Bone
Mr Daniel Bowden, Bideford, Devon
Corn House, Bowood Farm, Abbotsham, Bideford
The Cottage, Bowood Farm, Abbotsham, Bideford
Horseshoe Barn, Bowood Farm, Abbotsham, Bideford
M. and A. Bradburn, Westward Ho!
Graham John Braddick, Bideford
Mr Ian Braddick
Robert L.H. Braddick, Bideford

Mr Steven Braddick
Richard and Betty Bradford, Northam, Bideford
Chris and Linda Braund, Fremington
Chris Braund, Buckish
Mr H.J. (Bronc) Braunton
E.K. Breaks, Northam, Devon
Mr Fredrick Bright, Bideford, Devon
D. Broadribb, Bideford
Mr J.G. Bromhead, Littleham, Devon
R. Brooks
Carol Brown, Northam
Mr David Brown, Buckland Brewer
Mrs Jennifer L. Brown, Bideford, Devon
Sarah Brown, Bideford, Devon
John Brownrigg, Guildford, Surrey
Michael J. Bryant, Bideford, Devon
Tom Bryden, now in Southampton
Jack A. Burchell, Bideford, Devon
Mrs A. Burnage, Maidenhead, Berkshire
K.J. Burrow, Bucks Cross, Devon
Patricia M. Butler, Bideford, Devon
Henry Butterfield, Bideford, Devon
Mr Eric B. Cawsey
Mr M.J. Chance, Westward Ho!
Mr and Mrs R.T. Chapman
Roger and Paula Chapple, Hartland
Mr Percy W. Chubb
Margaret A. Church, Bideford, Devon
Joshua Ethan Clarke, Horns Cross
Tony Cliffe, Bideford
Wayne Clifton, Northam, Devon
Mabel A. Comer, Bideford, Devon
E.L. Coombs, Bideford, Devon
Flo Coombs, New Jersey, USA
W.A. Cork, formerly of Adjavin Farm, Bideford/now New Zealand
The Cork family, formerly of Adjavin Farm, Bideford
Barbara Cornford, Hallsannery
Mr K. and Mrs M. Coutts, Northam
J.A. Curtis, Westward Ho!, Devon
John F. Dainty, Bideford, Devon
Andrew John Daniel, Bideford, Devon

David J. Dark, Northam, Devon
John Dark, Bideford, Devon
Robert B. Dark
Susan M. Dart
J.C.C. David, Weare Giffard
Paul and Gill Dean, Bideford, Devon
Mr Peter C. Diwell
Winnifred E. Dockings
Christopher J. Drew, Bideford, Devon
Easterbrook, Bideford, Devon
Mrs Phyllis Eastman, Bideford
R.T. Edwards, Bideford
Geoffrey A. Ellam, Bideford, Devon
P.C. Elliott, Bideford, Devon
Eric Elston, Bideford
Alexander Ferriday
Danielle Filmer, Bideford
Mr and Mrs R. Filmer, Bideford
Paul Fisher, Vancouver Is., Canada
Eileen Ford, Bideford, Devon
Mrs S.F. Ford
Gail Foreshew (née Marlow), Abbotsham
Vivien R. Foster, Instow, Devon
Jeffrey Friendship, Bideford, Devon
Mrs Margaret L. Friendship
Peter S. Garner, Northam, Devon
Reginald T. Garner, Felpham, Sussex
Chris Garnett-Frizelle, Bideford, Devon
Cynthia D.N. Gibbons
Ian and Valerie Gibson, Northam, Devon
Michie Giddens, Bideford, Devon
Eric James Giddy, Bideford, Devon
Geoffrey James Giddy, Northam, Devon
Roger Michael Giddy, Appledore, Devon
Sarah Louise Giddy, Bideford, Devon
Tom Gillingham, Milton Damerel, Devon
Mike Glover, Bideford
Jack Gordon, Bideford
B.J. Gorrell, Bideford, Devon
Reginald C. Gorvett, Bideford, Devon
Michael B. Goss, Bideford, Devon
Bryan Goult, Halspill, Weare Giffard
William John Grant, Bideford, Devon
Mr R.J. and Mrs M.E. Greathead
S.R. Greaves
Sheila and Bob Griffin, Bideford, Devon
Mr W. and A.S. Griffiths, Bideford, Devon
Graham L.C. Gubb
Mr Neville J. Hackett, East-the-Water,
    Bideford, Devon
George and Linda Hadden, Westward Ho!

Frances Louise Haddock, Westward Ho!,
    Devon
Daniel Edward Hall, 17 March 1982 – 14
    May 2000
Gordon and Pauline Hammond,
    Appledore, North Devon
Terry, Linda, Elizabeth and Melinda
    Harding, Woolsery, Bideford
Peter George Harman, Bideford
Charles D. Harper, Instow
Arthur and Rosalyn Harris
David and Carol Harris, Lower Winsford,
    Bideford
William A.G. Harris, Bideford, Devon
Susan Hateley, Northam, Devon
Jack Hawkins, Bideford, Devon
Arthur Heal, March, Cambridgeshire
Nora Heard
Doreen Hearn, Northam, North Devon
Ken Hearn, Bideford
George Heath, Abbotsham
Mary Margaret Heath, Abbotsham
Sheila E.G. Henstridge
Mrs Barbara M. Hewis
Teresa J. Heywood, Buckland Brewer,
    Bideford, Devon
Robert H. Hicks
William J.C. Hilditch, Appledore, Devon
John Hillman
Mr and Mrs C.G. Hockin
Mr David Hocking, Appledore, North
    Devon
Lily J. Hocking, Appledore
Carol E. Hole, Bideford, Devon
Sandra E. Hole, Bideford, Devon
Mr Keith R. Holloway, Bideford, Devon
Anne Hulbert
Brenda Humphreys, Bideford, Devon
Yvonne Hurrell, Northam, Devon
Mary E. Husband
William Isaac, Queen Street, Bideford
Gordon H. Jackson, Buckland Brewer,
    Bideford
Sheila James, Bideford
Dorothy M. Jewell, Bideford, Devon
Mrs Phyllis Job, Northam, Devon
Richard Johns, Bideford, Devon
Mrs Ivy Johnson, Bideford, Devon
Brenda P.M. Jones, Appledore, Devon
Jean and Ray Jones, Bideford, Devon
Myra Jones, Littleham, Bideford

Mr and Mrs Malcolm Joy, Appledore, Devon
David E. Judd, Northam, Devon
Kate, Sarah and Tom, Northam
Albert Keen, Bideford, Devon
Mr Anthony C. Kelly, Northam, Bideford, Devon
Elizabeth Kelly, Bideford, Devon
Molly Kent, Bideford
Don G. Kersey, Bideford, Devon
Sanjay Khallie, Bideford, Devon
Brian J. Lacey, Bideford East
Alice M.V.M. Lamey, Bideford, Devon
Brian J. Lamey, Bideford, Devon
The Mayor and Residents of Landivisiau
Robert W.J. Langmead, Bideford, Devon
Alison Langstone-Gabell, Woolsery, Devon
Mark J. Lavington, Appledore, Devon
Mrs K.M. Lawrence, Bideford, Devon
Kirrin Lee Palmer, Bideford, Devon
David and Margaret Ley, Bideford
Mr Terry Limb, Bideford
Mr Graham Little, Bideford, Devon
Dr and Mrs Ragaii Loka, Abbotsham, Bideford, Devon
Eileen B. Mann, Instow, Devon
Philip and Gill Marlow, Abbotsham
Richard Marlow, Abbotsham
L. and S. Martin, Orchard Farm, Monkleigh
Peter L.F. Martin, Northam, Devon
Joy Mason, Bideford, Devon
Dr Kit Mayers, Instow
Mrs Margaret Mayne, Appledore, Devon
Keith J. McBride, Northam, Devon
Mr T. McKenzie, Bideford, Devon
D.A.G. Metherell, Bideford
Dr and Mrs David Milburn, Abbotsham, Bideford, Devon
Amy and John Mitchell
Jennie Moffatt, Abbotsham
W. Herbert Molland
Philip Molyneux Esq., Northam, North Devon
David Stanley Morris, Bideford, Devon
Richard Stanley Morris, Bideford, Devon
Mr A. Mugford and Miss J. Heath, Bideford, Devon
Alex Munro-Chick, Northam
John and Gillian Murtagh, Bideford, Devon
Bob Muschamp, Northam, Devon
John Nicholls, Northam, Bideford

Stanley J. Nichols, Bideford, Devon
Albie Nickels, Weare Giffard
M. Northcott, Teapot House, Northam
Michael Oke
Anthony Ivor Osborne, Bideford, Devon
Colin Paddon, Walton-on-Thames, Surrey
Martyn Paddon, Shirley, Croydon
Neil Paddon, Bideford, North Devon
Pam Paddon, Sunnyside, Bideford
Fred A. Palmer, Bideford, Devon
Terry and Carol Palmer, Bideford
Mervyn T. Parish, Bideford, Devon
Simon Parsons, Chipping Sodbury
Sue Parsons, Appledore, Devon
J. and C. Pascoe, Bideford, Devon
Patricia Pate
Muriel Patt, Bideford, Devon
B.D. Pidgeon, Bideford, North Devon
Barbara Piper, Bideford, Devon
Clive and Jill Piper, Bideford
Nicholas and Sarah Piper, Tamerton Foliot, Plymouth
Judith and Alan Poole, Ashridge, Horwood
Mr and Mrs M.T. Poole, Littleham, Nr Bideford
Caroline Prince, Thorverton, Devon
Victoria Prince, Eastington, Gloucestershire
Alice and Ken Prust, formerly Marsh Farm
Raymond George Quick, Bideford, Devon
Lennie Rawle, Appledore, Devon
M. Raymont, Bideford
Paul T.M. Reeves, Bideford
Mr and Mrs A. Rickard, Bideford, Devon
Bernard and Linda Ridd, Bideford
Jennifer A. Rowe, Bideford, Devon
Graham and Jenny Rowland, Bideford
Miss Grace R. Rundle, Bideford, Devon
Margaret R. Russell, Bideford
Jan and Mike Sanders, Bideford, Devon
Ruth Elizabeth Sanders
Mr S. Sanders, Bideford
Paul and Jennifer Sargent, Bideford, Devon
James and Carol Saumarez, Bideford, Devon
Mrs Carole A. Sawbridge, Bideford, Devon
Mr and Mrs F.C. Sawle
Mr and Mrs I.J. Sawle
Mike and Pam Schiller, Bideford, Devon
Graeme L. Scott, Bideford, Devon
Anthony J. Screech, Bideford, Devon
Mark J. Screech, Bideford, Devon

Les and Dawn Seatherton
Liz Shakespeare and Steve Tremain, Littleham, Bideford
M.J. and E. Sherborne
John F. Short, Bideford, Devon
Mrs Elsie Shute (101 years old), Bideford
S.J. Shute, Bideford, Devon
Paul Simpson
Mr Martyn Andrew Slade, Bideford, Devon
Brian Slee, Bucks Cross, Devon
Derrick B. Slee, Bideford, North Devon
David Sloman, Saltrens, Monkleigh, Bideford
Rita Sluman, Bideford
Frank and Ruby Sluman, Bideford
Dawn Smith, Ford, Bideford
Mr and Mrs W.J. Smith, Bowden Green, Bideford, Devon
Susan A. Spencer, Bideford, Devon
Ronald Squire, Bideford, Devon
Caroline Corrol Stansfield, Instow
Mr and Mrs C. Stapleton, Bideford, Devon
Wilfred John Steer, Instow
Joyce Stevens, Bideford, North Devon
John and Dawn Stone, Australia
Malcolm and Barbara Stone, Bideford
Colin M. Sturdy
Mrs Joyce Tanton (née Vine), Bideford
Helen M. Tate, Bideford, Devon
John and Angela Taylor, Bideford, Devon
Mr John R. Taylor, Bideford, Devon
Rosemary Susan Taylor, Westward Ho!
David Thisby, Hexam, Northumberland
Michael and Karen Thurlow, Londonderry Farm, Bideford
Edith Tibbles, Northam

Pat Tillinghast, Mandurah, West Australia
Vernon Tomkins, Bideford, Devon
Brian Trick, Bideford, Devon
Mr Frederick Tucker, Bideford. 26.6.18.
John Knight Turner
Leonard Turner, Northam, Devon
Mr W.H. Unett
Mark Upton, Bideford, Devon
Professor and Mrs M.P. Vessey, Fulbrook, Oxon
C.B. and S.A. Waldon, Bideford
M. Walker, Bideford, Devon
John F.W. Walling, Newton Abbot, Devon
Colin Walters (In Memory of), Bideford
Doreen M. Walters
Chris Watkins, Bideford, North Devon
Barbara and Robert Webb, Bideford
Joyce Webb (Gifford), Bideford
Jim Weeks, Bideford, Devon
Dawn Wheeler, Bideford, Devon
Mrs Janet Wicks (née Braddick)
Colin J. Wilkey, Westward Ho!
Mr Reginald A. Williams, Bideford, Devon
A. and H.F. Wills, Annery Kiln, Devon
Major R.E. Willsher, Bideford, Devon
D. Withall, Bideford
Martyn J. Wonnacott, Horns Cross, Bideford
Jim and Margaret Wood, Bideford, Devon
Sue and Ray Woods, Burgess Hill, West Sussex
Queenie M. Woolland, Bideford, Devon
Mr G.A. Wren, Bath
Mr W.P.J. Wren, Bideford, Devon
Caroline Wright, Bideford, Devon
Michele M. Wright, June 2004
Valerie A. Yeates, Bideford, Devon

In order to include as many historical photographs as possible in this volume, a printed index is not included. However, the Devon titles in the Community History Series are indexed by Genuki.

For further information and indexes to various volumes in the series, please visit: http://www.cs.ncl.ac.uk/genuki/DEV/indexingproject.html